HISTORY

OF

HORTENSE,

DAUGHTER OF JOSEPHINE, QUEEN OF HOLLAND,
MOTHER OF NAPOLEON III.

BY

JOHN S. C. ABBOTT

With Illustrations

Sandycroft Publishing

History of Hortense

Daughter of Josephine, Queen of Holland,
Mother of Napoleon III

By John S. C. Abbott

First published 1870

This edition ©2017

Sandycroft Publishing

http://sandycroftpublishing.com

ISBN 978-1542956017

CONTENTS

Preface..i
Chapter I: Parentage and Birth..1
Chapter II: The Marriage of Josephine and General Bonaparte......18
Chapter III: Hortense and Duroc..34
Chapter IV: The Marriage of Hortense..49
Chapter V: Birth of Louis Napoleon and the Divorce of
    Josephine..69
Chapter VI: The Death of Josephine...84
Chapter VII: The Sorrows of Exile...101
Chapter VIII: Peaceful Days, yet Sad..115
Chapter IX: Life at Arenemberg..141
Chapter X: Letter from Louis Napoleon to His Mother..............155
Chapter XI: The Death of Hortense, and the Enthronement of
    her Son..174

ILLUSTRATIONS

Hortense..ii
Josephine taking leave of her children.......................................12
The reconciliation...31
The love letter..46
The little Prince Charles Napoleon..58
The divorce announced..78
The death of Madame Broc..92
Hortense and her children...105
Hortense at Arenemberg..119
Interview in the Coliseum..130
The study of Louis Napoleon...148
The arrest...163

PREFACE

THE French Revolution was perhaps as important an event as has occurred in the history of nations. It was a drama in three acts. The first was the Revolution itself, properly so called, with its awful scenes of terror and of blood—the exasperated millions struggling against the accumulated oppression of ages.

The second act in the drama was the overthrow of the Directory by Napoleon, and the introduction of the Consulate and the Empire; the tremendous struggle against the combined dynasties of Europe; the demolition of the Empire, and the renewed crushing of the people by the triumph of the nobles and the kings.

Then came the third act in the drama—perhaps the last, perhaps not—in which the French people again drove out the Bourbons, re-established the Republican Empire, with its principle of equal rights for all, and placed upon the throne the heir of the great Emperor.

No man can understand the career of Napoleon I without being acquainted with those scenes of anarchy and terror which preceded his reign. No man can understand the career of Napoleon III unless familiar with the struggle of the people against the despots in the Revolution, their triumph in the Empire, their defeat in its overthrow, and their renewed triumph in its restoration.

Hortense was intimately associated with all these scenes. Her father fell beneath the slide of the guillotine; her mother was imprisoned and doomed to die; and she and her brother were turned penniless into the streets. By the marriage of her mother with Napoleon, she became the daughter of the Emperor, and one of the most brilliant and illustrious ladies of the imperial court. The triumph of the Allies sent her into exile, where her influence and her instruction prepared her son to contribute powerfully to the restoration of the Empire, and to reign with ability which is admired by his friends and acknowledged by his foes. The mother of Napoleon III never allowed her royally-endowed son to forget, even in the gloomiest days of exile and of sorrow, that it might yet be his privilege to re-establish the Republican Empire, and to restore the dynasty of the people from its overthrow by the despotic Allies.

Hortense.

In this brief record of the life of one who experienced far more than the usual vicissitudes of humanity, whose career was one of the saddest upon record, and who ever exhibited virtues which won the enthusiastic love of all who knew her, the writer has admitted nothing which cannot be sustained by incontrovertible evidence, and has suppressed nothing sustained by any testimony worthy of a moment's respect. This history will show that Hortense had her faults. Who is without them? There are not many, however, who will read these pages without profound admiration for the character of one of the noblest of women, and without finding the eye often dimmed, in view of her heartrending griefs.

HORTENSE

Chapter I
Parentage and Birth

In the year 1776 a very beautiful young lady, by the name of Josephine Rose Tascher, was crossing the Atlantic Ocean from the island of Martinique to France. She was but fifteen years of age; and, having been left an orphan in infancy, had been tenderly reared by an uncle and aunt, who were wealthy, being proprietors of one of the finest plantations upon the island. Josephine was accompanied upon the voyage by her uncle. She was the betrothed of a young French nobleman by the name of Viscount Alexander de Beauharnais, who had recently visited Martinique, and who owned several large estates adjoining the property which Josephine would probably inherit.

It was with great reluctance that Josephine yielded to the importunities of her friends and accepted the proffered hand of the viscount. Her affections had long been fixed upon a playmate of her childhood by the name of William, and her love was passionately returned. William was then absent in France, pursuing his education. De Beauharnais was what would usually be called a very splendid man. He was of high rank, young, rich, intelligent, and fascinating in his manners. The marriage of Josephine with the viscount would unite the properties. Her friends, in their desire to accomplish the union, cruelly deceived Josephine. They intercepted the letters of William, and withheld her letters to him, and represented to her that William, amidst the gaieties of Paris, had proved a false lover, and had entirely forgotten her. De Beauharnais, attracted by the grace and beauty of Josephine, had ardently offered her his hand. Under these circumstances the inexperienced maiden had consented to the union, and was now crossing the Atlantic with her uncle for the consummation of the nuptials in France.

Upon her arrival she was conducted to Fontainebleau, where De Beauharnais hastened to meet her. Proud of her attractions, he took great pleasure in introducing her to his highborn friends, and lavished upon her every attention. Josephine was grateful, but sad, for her heart still yearned for William. Soon William, hearing of her arrival, and not knowing of her engagement, anxiously repaired to Fontainebleau. The interview was agonizing. William still loved her with the utmost devotion. They both found that they had been the victims of a conspiracy, though one of which De Beauharnais had no knowledge.

Josephine, young, inexperienced, far from home, and surrounded by the wealthy and powerful friends of her betrothed, had gone too far in the arrangements for the marriage to recede. Her anguish, however, was so great that she was thrown into a violent fever. She had no friend to whom she could confide her emotions. But in most affecting tones she entreated that her marriage might be delayed for a few months until she should regain her health. Her friends consented, and she took refuge for a time in the Convent of Panthemont, under the tender care of the sisters.

It is not probable that De Beauharnais was at all aware of the real state of Josephine's feelings. He was proud of her, and loved her as truly as a fashionable man of the world could love. It is also to be remembered that at that time in France it was not customary for young ladies to have much influence in the choice of their husbands. It was supposed that their parents could much more judiciously arrange these matters than the young ladies themselves.

Josephine was sixteen years of age at the time of her marriage. Her attractions were so remarkable that she immediately became a great favorite at the French court, to which the rank of her husband introduced her. Marie Antoinette was then the youthful bride of Louis XVI. She was charmed with Josephine, and lavished upon her the most flattering attentions. Two children were born of this marriage, both of whom attained worldwide renown. The first was a son, Eugene. He was born in September, 1781. His career was very elevated, and he occupied with distinguished honor all the lofty positions to which he was raised. He became duke of Leuchtenberg, prince of Eichstedt, viceroy of Italy. He married the Princess Augusta, daughter of the King of Bavaria.

"Prince Eugene, under a simple exterior, concealed a noble character and great talents. Honor, integrity, humanity, and love of order and justice were the principal traits of his character. Wise in the council, undaunted in the field, and moderate in the exercise of power, he never appeared greater than in the midst of reverses, as the events of 1813 and 1814 prove. He was inaccessible to the spirit of party, benevolent and beneficent, and more devoted to the good of others than his own."[1]

The second child was a daughter, Hortense, the subject of this brief memoir. She was born on the 10th of January, 1783. In the opening scenes of that most sublime of earthly tragedies, the French Revolution, M. de Beauharnais espoused the popular cause, though of noble blood, and though his elder brother, the Marquis de Beauharnais, earnestly advocated the cause of the king and the court.

The entire renunciation of the Christian religion was then popular in France. Alexander de Beauharnais, like most of his young pleasure-loving companions, was an infidel. His conduct soon became such that the heart of poor Josephine was quite broken. Her two children, Eugene and Hortense, both inherited the affectionate and gentle traits of their mother, and were her only solace. In her anguish she unguardedly wrote to her friends in Martinique, who had almost forced her into her connection with Beauharnais:

"Were it not for my children, I should, without a pang, renounce France forever. My duty requires me to forget William. And yet, if *we* had been united together, I should not today have been troubling you with my griefs."

Viscount Beauharnais chanced to see this letter. It roused his jealousy fearfully. A sense of "honor" would allow him to lavish his attentions upon guilty favorites, while that same sense of "honor" would urge him to wreak vengeance upon his unhappy, injured wife, because, in her neglect and anguish, with no false, but only a true affection, her memory turned to the loved companion of her childhood. According to the standard of the fashionable world, Beauharnais was a very honorable man. According to the standard of Christianity, he was a sinner in the sight of God, and was to answer for this conduct at the final judgment.

He reproached his wife in the severest language of denunciation. He took from her her son Eugene. He applied to the courts for a divorce, demanding his daughter Hortense also. Josephine pleaded with him in vain, for the sake of their children, not to proclaim their

---
[1] *Encyclopædia Americana.*

disagreement to the world. Grief-stricken, poor Josephine retired to a convent to await the trial. The verdict was triumphantly in her favor. But her heart was broken. She was separated from her husband, though the legal tie was not severed.

Her friends in Martinique, informed of these events, wrote, urging her to return to them. She decided to accept the invitation. Hortense was with her mother. M. de Beauharnais had sent Eugene, whom he had taken from her, to a boarding school. Before sailing for Martinique she obtained an interview with M. de Beauharnais, and with tears entreated that she might take Eugene with her also. He was unrelenting; Josephine, with a crushed and world-weary heart, folded Hortense to her bosom, then an infant but three years of age, and returned to her tropical home, which she had sadly left but a few years before. Here, on the retired plantation, soothed by the sympathy of her friends, she strove to conceal her anguish.

There was never a more loving heart than that with which Josephine was endowed. She clung to Hortense with tenderness which has rarely been equaled. They were always together. During the day Hortense was ever by her side, and at night she nestled in her mother's bosom. Living amidst the scenes of tropical luxuriance and beauty, endeared to her by the memories of childhood, Josephine could almost have been happy but for the thoughts of her absent Eugene. Grief for her lost child preyed ever upon her heart.

Her alienated husband, relieved from all restraint, plunged anew into those scenes of fashionable dissipation for which Paris was then renowned. But sickness, sorrows, and misfortunes came. In those dark hours he found that no earthly friend can supply the place of a virtuous and loving wife. He wrote to her, expressing bitter regret for his conduct, and imploring her to return. The wounds which Josephine had received were too deep to be easily healed. Forgiving as she was by nature, she said to her friends that the memory of the past was so painful that, were it not for Eugene, she should very much prefer not to return to France again, but to spend the remainder of her days in the seclusion of her native island. Her friends did everything in their power to dissuade her from returning. But a mother's love for her son triumphed, and with Hortense she took ship for France.

An event occurred upon this voyage which is as instructive as it is interesting. Many years afterwards, when Josephine was Empress of France, and the wealth of the world was almost literally at her feet, on one occasion some young ladies who were visiting the court requested Josephine to show them her diamonds. These jewels were almost of priceless value, and were kept in a vault, the keys of which were confided to the most trusty persons. Josephine, who seldom wore jewels, very amiably complied with their request. A large table was brought into the saloon. Her maids in waiting brought in a great number of caskets, of every size and form, containing the precious gems.

As these caskets were opened, they were dazzled with the brilliancy, the size, and the number of these ornaments. The different sets composed probably by far the most brilliant collection in Europe. In Napoleon's conquering career, the cities which he had entered lavished their gifts upon Josephine. The most remarkable of these jewels consisted of large white diamonds. There were others in the shape of pears formed of pearls of the richest colors. There were opals, rubies, sapphires, and emeralds of such marvelous value that the large diamonds that encircled them were considered as mere mountings not regarded in the estimation made of the value of the jewels.

As the ladies gazed upon the splendor of this collection, they were lost in wonder and admiration. Josephine, after enjoying for a while their expressions of delight, and having allowed them to examine the beautiful gems thoroughly, said to them kindly:

"I had no other motive, in ordering my jewels to be opened before you, than to spoil your fancy for such ornaments. After having seen such splendid sets, you can never feel a wish for inferior ones; the less so when you reflect how unhappy I have been, although with so rare a collection at my command. During the first dawn of my extraordinary elevation, I delighted in these trifles, many of which were presented to me in Italy. I grew by degrees so tired of them that I no longer wear any, except when I am in some respects compelled to do so by my new rank in the world. A thousand accidents may, besides, contribute to deprive me of these brilliant, though useless objects. Do I not possess the pendants of Queen Marie Antoinette? And yet am I quite sure of retaining them? Trust to me, ladies, and do not envy a splendor which does not constitute happiness. I shall not fail to surprise you when I relate that I once felt more pleasure at receiving an old pair of shoes than at being presented with all the diamonds which are now spread before you."

The young ladies could not help smiling at this observation, persuaded as they were that Josephine was not in earnest. But she repeated her assertions in so serious a manner that they felt the utmost curiosity to hear the story of this *wonderful pair of shoes*.

"I repeat it, ladies," said her majesty, "it is strictly true, that the present which, of all others, has afforded me most pleasure was a pair of old shoes of the coarsest leather; and you will readily believe it when you have heard my story.

"I had set sail from Martinique, with Hortense, on board a ship in which we received such marked attentions that they are indelibly impressed on my memory. Being separated from my first husband, my pecuniary resources were not very flourishing. The expense of my return to France, which the state of my affairs rendered necessary, had nearly drained me of everything, and I found great difficulty in making the purchases which were indispensably requisite for the voyage. Hortense, who was a smart, lively child, sang negro songs, and performed negro dances with admirable accuracy. She was the delight of the sailors, and, in return for their fondness, she made them her favorite company. I no sooner fell asleep than she slipped upon deck and rehearsed her various little exercises, to the renewed delight and admiration of all on board.

"An old mate was particularly fond of her, and whenever he found a moment's leisure from his daily occupations, he devoted it to his little friend, who was also exceedingly attached to him. My daughter's shoes were soon worn out with her constant dancing and skipping. Knowing as she did that I had no other pair for her, and fearing lest I should prevent her going upon deck if I should discover the plight of those she was fast wearing away, she concealed the trifling accident from my knowledge. I saw her once returning with bleeding feet, and asked her, in the utmost alarm, if she had hurt herself; 'No, mamma.' 'But your feet are bleeding.' 'It really is nothing.' I insisted upon ascertaining what ailed her, and found that her shoes were all in tatters, and her flesh dreadfully torn by a nail.

"We had as yet only performed half the voyage; a long time would necessarily elapse before I could procure a fresh pair of shoes; I was mortified at the bare anticipation of the distress my poor Hortense would feel at being compelled to remain confined in my wretched little cabin, and of the injury her health might experience from the want of exercise. At the moment when I was wrapped up in sorrow, and giving free vent to my tears, our friend the mate made his appearance, and inquired, with his honest bluntness, the cause of our *whimperings*. Hortense replied, in a sobbing voice, that she could no longer go upon deck because she had torn her shoes, and I had no others to give her.

" 'Is that all?' said the sailor.' I have an old pair in my trunk; let me go for them. You, madame, will cut them up, and I shall sew them over again to the best of my power; everything on board ship shall be turned to account; this is not the place for being too nice or particular; we have our most important wants gratified when we have the needful.'

"He did not wait for our reply, but went in quest of his old shoes, which he brought to us with an air of exultation, and offered them to Hortense, who received the gift with every demonstration of delight.

"We set to work with the greatest alacrity, and my daughter was enabled, towards the close of the day, to enjoy the pleasure of again amusing the ship's company. I repeat it, that no present was ever received by me with more sincere gratitude. I greatly reproach myself for having neglected to make inquiries after the worthy seaman, who was only known on board by the name of James. I should have felt a sincere satisfaction in rendering him some service, since it was afterwards in my power to do so."

Josephine had spent three years in Martinique. Consequently, upon her return to France, Hortense was six years of age. Soon after her arrival the Reign of Terror commenced. The guillotine was erected, and its knife was busy beheading those who were suspected of not being in full sympathy with the reformers whom revolution had brought into power. Though Viscount Beauharnais had earnestly espoused the popular cause; though he had been president of the National Assembly, and afterwards general of the Army of the Rhine, still he was of noble birth, and his older brother was an aristocrat, and an emigrant. He was consequently suspected, and arrested. Having conducted him to prison, a committee of the Convention called at the residence of Josephine to examine the children, hoping to extort from them some evidence against their father. Josephine, in a letter to her aunt, thus describes this singular scene:

> "You would hardly believe, dear aunt, that my children have just undergone a long and minute examination. That

wicked old man, the member of the committee whom I have already mentioned to you, called upon me, and, affecting to feel uneasy in regard to my husband, and to converse with me respecting him, opened a conversation with my children. I acknowledge that I at first fell into the snare. What surprised me, however, was the sudden affability of the man. But he soon betrayed himself by the malignity and even bitterness which he displayed when the children replied in such a manner as to give him no advantage over their unhappy parents. I soon penetrated his artful intentions.

"When he found me on my guard, he threw off the mask, and admitted that he was desired to procure information from my children, which, he said, might be more relied on, as it would bear the stamp of candor. He then entered into a formal examination. At that moment I felt an indescribable emotion; and the conflicting effects of fear, anger, and indignation alternately agitated me. I was even upon the point of openly giving vent to my feelings against the hoary revolutionist, when I reflected that I might, by so doing, materially injure M. de Beauharnais, against whom that atrocious villain appeared to have vowed perpetual enmity. I accordingly checked my angry passions. He desired me to leave him alone with my children; I attempted to resist, but his ferocious glance compelled me to give way.

"He confined Hortense in the closet, and began to put questions to her brother. My daughter's turn came next. As for this child, in whom he discovered a premature quickness and penetration far above her age, he kept questioning her for a great length of time. After having sounded them respecting our common topics of conversation, our opinions, the visits and letters we were in the habit of receiving, but more particularly the occurrences they might have witnessed, he came to the main point—I mean, to the expressions used by Alexander. My children gave very proper replies; such, in fact, as were suited to their respective dispositions. And notwithstanding the artfulness of a mischievous man whose object is to discover guilt, the frankness of my son and the quick penetration of my daughter disconcerted his low cunning, and even defeated the object he had in view."

Parentage and Birth

Viscount Beauharnais, when arrested, was conveyed to the palace of the Luxembourg, where he was imprisoned with many other captives. To spare the feelings of the children, the fact of his imprisonment was concealed from them by Josephine, and they were given to understand that their father, not being very well, had placed himself under the care of a celebrated physician, who had recommended him to take up his residence at the Luxembourg, where there was much vacant space, and consequently purer air. The imprisoned father was very anxious to see his wife and children. The authorities consented, allowing the children to go in first under the care of an attendant, and afterwards their mother.

Hortense, child as she was, was bewildered by the scene, and her suspicions were evidently excited. As she came out, she said to her mother, "I think papa's apartments are very small, and the patients are very numerous."

After the children had left, Josephine was introduced. She knew that her husband's life was in imminent peril. His penitence and grateful love had produced entire reconciliation, and had won back Josephine's heart. She was not willing that the children should witness the tender and affecting interview which, under such circumstances, must take place.

Beauharnais had but little hope that he should escape the guillotine. As Josephine, bathed in tears, rushed into his arms, all his fortitude forsook him. His emotion was so great that his wife, struggling against her own anguish, used her utmost endeavors to calm and console him.

In the midst of this heartrending scene, to their consternation, the children, by some misunderstanding, were again led into the apartment. The father and mother struggled to disguise from them the cause of that emotion which they could not conceal. For a time the children were silent and bewildered; then Hortense, though with evident misgivings, attempted to console her parents. The events of her saddened life had rendered her unusually precocious. Turning to her mother, she begged her not to give way to so much sorrow, assuring her that she could not think that her father was dangerously ill. Then addressing Eugene, she said, in a peculiar tone which her parents felt as a reproach,

"I do not think, brother, that papa is very sick. At any rate, it is not such a sickness as doctors can cure." Josephine felt the reproach, and conscious that it was in some degree deserved, said:

"What do you mean, my child? Do you think your father and I have combined to deceive you?"

"Pardon me, mamma, but I do think so."

"Oh, sister," exclaimed Eugene, "how can you speak so strangely?"

"On the contrary," Hortense replied, "it is very plain and natural. Surely affectionate parents may be allowed to deceive their children when they wish to spare their feelings."

Josephine was seated in the lap of her husband. Hortense sprang into her mother's arms, and encircled the neck of both father and mother in a loving embrace. Eugene caught the contagion, and by his tears and affecting caresses added to this domestic scene of love and woe.

It is the universal testimony that Eugene and Hortense were so lovely in person and in character that they instantly won the affection of all who saw them. The father was conscious that he was soon to die. He knew that all his property would be confiscated. It was probable that Josephine would also be led to her execution. The guillotine spared neither sex who had incurred the suspicions of enthroned democracy. Both parents forgot themselves, in their anxiety for their children. The execution of Beauharnais would undoubtedly lead to the arrest and execution of Josephine. The property of the condemned was invariably confiscated. There was thus danger that the children would be turned in beggary into the streets. It is difficult to conceive the anguish which must have rent the hearts of affectionate parents in hours of woe so awful.

The prisons were crowded with victims. Brief as were the trials, and rapid as was the execution of the guillotine, there was some considerable delay before Beauharnais was led before the revolutionary tribunal. In the meantime Josephine made several calls, with her children, upon her imprisoned husband. Little Hortense, whose suspicions were strongly excited, watched every word, and soon became so convinced that her father was a prisoner that it became impossible for her parents any longer to conceal the fact.

"What has papa done," inquired Hortense, "that they will not let him come home?"

"He has done nothing wrong," said Josephine, timidly, for she knew not what spies might be listening. "He is only accused of being unfriendly to the Government."

Holding the hand of Eugene, Hortense exclaimed impetuously, "Oh, we will punish your accusers as soon as we are strong enough."

"Be silent, my child," said her father anxiously. "If you are overheard I am lost. Both your mother and I may be made to suffer for any imprudent remark which you may make."

"But, papa, have you not often told us," said Eugene, "that it was proper to resist an act of oppression?"

"Yes," said the father proudly, though conscious that his words might be reported and misrepresented to his merciless judges. "And I repeat it. Our conduct, however, must be guided by rules of prudence; and whoever attempts to defeat the views of tyranny must beware of awaking it from its slumbers."

No philosophy has yet been able to explain the delicate mechanism of the human soul; its fleeting and varying emotions of joy and sadness, its gleams of hope and shades of despair come and go, controlled by influences which entirely elude human scrutiny. In these days of gloom, rays of hope occasionally penetrated the cell of Beauharnais.

At last the hour of dread came. Beauharnais was led before the terrible tribunal. He was falsely accused of having promoted the surrender of Mentz to the Allies. He was doomed to death, and was sent to the Conciergerie, whence he was to be conducted to his execution. This was in July, 1794. Beauharnais was then thirty-four years of age.

It seems that the conversation which we have reported as having taken place in the cell of Beauharnais had been overheard by listening ears, and reported to the committee as a conspiracy for the overthrow of the Republic. The arrest of Josephine was ordered. A warning letter from some friend reached her a few moments before the officers arrived, urging her to fly. It was an early hour in the morning. There was little sleep for Josephine amidst those scenes of terror, and she was watching by the side of her slumbering children. What could she do? Should she abandon her children, and seek to save her own life by flight? A mother's love rendered that impossible. Should she take them with her in her flight? That would render her arrest certain; and the fact of her attempting to escape would be urged as evidence of her guilt.

While distracted with these thoughts, the clatter of armed men was heard at her door. With anguish which none but a mother

Josephine taking leave of her children.

Parentage and Birth

can comprehend, she bent over her children and imprinted, as she supposed, a last kiss upon their cheeks. The affectionate little Hortense, though asleep, was evidently agitated by troubled dreams. As she felt the imprint of her mother's lips, she threw her arms around her neck and exclaimed, "Come to bed, dear mamma; they shall not take you away tonight. I have prayed to God for you."

Josephine, to avoid waking the children, stepped softly from the room, closed the door, and entered her parlor. Here she was rudely seized by the soldiers, who regarded her as a hated aristocrat. They took possession of the house and all its furniture in the name of the Republic, left the children to suffer or to die as fate might decide, and dragged the mother to imprisonment in the Convent of the Carmelites.

When the children awoke in the morning, they found themselves alone and friendless in the heart of Paris. The wonderful events of their lives thus far had rendered them both unusually precocious. Eugene in particular seemed to be endowed with all the thoughtfulness and wisdom of a full-grown man. After a few moments of anguish and tears, in view of their dreadful situation, they sat down to deliberate upon the course to be pursued. Hortense suggested that they should repair to the Luxembourg and seek the protection of their father in his imprisonment there. But Eugene, apprehensive that such a step might in some way compromise the safety of their father, recalled to mind that they had a great-aunt, far advanced in life, who was residing at Versailles in deep retirement. He proposed that they should seek refuge with her. Finding a former domestic of the family, she kindly led them to their aunt, where the desolate children were tenderly received.

Beauharnais was now in the Conciergerie, doomed to die, and awaiting his execution. Josephine was in the prison of the Carmelites, expecting hourly to be led to the tribunal to receive also her doom of death.

Hortense, an affectionate child, ardent and unreflecting in her impatience to see her mother, one morning left her aunt's house at Fontainebleau, to which place her aunt had removed, and in a market-cart traveled thirty miles to Paris. Here the energetic child, impelled by grief and love, succeeded in finding her mother's maid, Victorine. It was however impossible for them to obtain access to the prison, and Hortense the next day returned to Fontainebleau.

Josephine, upon being informed of this imprudent act, to which affection had impelled her child, wrote to her the following letter:

"I should be entirely satisfied with the good heart of my Hortense, were I not displeased with her bad head. How is it, my daughter, that, without permission from your aunt, you have come to Paris? 'But it was to see me, you will say.' You ought to be aware that no one can see me without an order, to obtain which requires both means and precautions. And besides, you got upon M. Dorset's cart, at the risk of incommoding him, and retarding the conveyance of his merchandise. In all this you have been very inconsiderate. My child, observe: it is not sufficient to do good, you must also do good properly. At your age, the first of all virtues is confidence and docility towards your relations. I am therefore obliged to tell you that I prefer your tranquil attachment to your misplaced warmth. This, however, does not prevent me from embracing you, but less tenderly than I shall do when I learn that you have returned to your aunt."

On the evening of the 24th of July M. de Beauharnais received the announcement in his cell, that with the dawn of the next morning he was to be led to the guillotine. Under these circumstances he wrote the following farewell letter to his wife:

"I have yet a few minutes to devote to affection, tears, and regret, and then I must wholly give myself up to the glory of my fate and to thoughts of immortality. When you receive this letter, my dear Josephine, your husband will have ceased to live, and will be tasting true existence in the bosom of his Creator. Do not weep for him. The wicked and senseless beings who survive him are more worthy of your tears, for they are doing mischief which they can never repair. But let us not cloud the present moments by any thoughts of their guilt. I wish, on the contrary, to brighten these hours by the reflection that I have enjoyed the affection of a lovely woman, and that our union would have been an uninterrupted course of happiness, but for errors which I was too late to acknowledge and atone for. This thought wrings tears from

Parentage and Birth

my eyes, though your generous heart pardons me. But this is no time to revive the recollection of my errors and of your wrongs. What thanks I owe to Providence, who will reward you.

"That Providence disposes of me before my time. This is another blessing, for which I am grateful. Can a virtuous man live happy when he sees the whole world a prey to the wicked? I should rejoice in being taken away, were it not for the thought of leaving those I love behind me. But if the thoughts of the dying are presentiments, something in my heart tells me that these horrible butcheries are drawing to a close; that the executioners will, in their turn, become victims; that the arts and sciences will again flourish in France; that wise and moderate laws will take the place of cruel sacrifices, and that you will at length enjoy the happiness which you have deserved. Our children will discharge the debt for their father.

"I resume these incoherent and almost illegible lines, which were interrupted by the entrance of my jailer. I have submitted to a cruel ceremony, which, under any other circumstances, I would have resisted at the sacrifice of my life. Yet why should we rebel against necessity? Reason tells us to make the best of it we can. My hair has been cut off. I had some idea of buying a part of it, in order to leave to my wife and children an unequivocal pledge of my last recollection of them. Alas! my heart breaks at the very thought, and my tears bedew the paper on which I am writing. Adieu, all that I love. Think of me, and do not forget that to die the victim of tyrants and the martyrs of liberty sheds luster on the scaffold."

Josephine did not receive this letter until after her husband's execution. The next afternoon one of the daily papers was brought into the prison of the Carmelites. Josephine anxiously ran her eye over the record of the executions, and found the name of her husband in the fatal list. She fell senseless to the floor in a long-continued swoon. When consciousness returned, she exclaimed at first, in the delirium of her anguish, "O God, let me die! let me die! There is no peace for me but in the grave." And then again a mother's love, as she thought of her orphan children, led her to cling to the misery of existence for their sake. Soon, however, the unpitying agents of the revolutionary tribunal came to her with the announcement that in two days she was to be led to the Conciergerie, and thence to her execution.

In the following letter Josephine informed her children of the death of their father, and of her own approaching execution. It is a letter highly characteristic of this wonderful woman in the attempt, by the assumption of calmness, to avoid as far as possible lacerating the feelings of Eugene and Hortense.

> "The hand which will deliver this to you is faithful and sure. You will receive it from a friend who knows and has shared my sorrows. I know not by what accident she has hitherto been spared. I call this accident fortunate; she regards it as a calamity. 'Is it not disgraceful to live,' said she yesterday, 'when all who are good have the honor of dying?' May Heaven, as the reward of her courage, refuse her the fatal honor she desires.
>
> "As to me, I am qualified for that honor, and I am preparing myself for receiving it. Why has disease spared me so long? But I must not murmur. As a wife, I ought to follow the fate of my husband, and can there now be any fate more glorious than to ascend the scaffold? It is a patent of immortality, purchased by a prompt and pleasing death.
>
> "My children, your father is dead, and your mother is about to follow him. But as before that final stroke the assassins leave me a few moments to myself, I wish to employ them in writing to you. Socrates, when condemned, philosophized with his disciples. A mother, on the point of undergoing a similar fate, may discourse with her children.
>
> "My last sigh will be for you, and I wish to make my last words a lasting lesson. Time was, when I gave you lessons in a more pleasing way. But the present will not be the less useful, that it is given at so serious a moment. I have the weakness to water it with my tears. I shall soon have the courage to seal it with my blood.
>
> "Hitherto it was impossible to be happier than I have been. While to my union with your father I owed my felicity, I may venture to think and to say that to my character I was

indebted for that union. I found in my heart the means of winning the affection of my husband's relations. Patience and gentleness always succeed in gaining the goodwill of others. You also, my dear children, possess natural advantages which cost little, and are of great value. But you must learn how to employ them, and that is what I still feel a pleasure in teaching you by my example.

"Here I must record the gratitude I owe to my excellent brother-in-law, who has, under various circumstances, given me proofs of the most sincere friendship, though he was of quite a different opinion from your father, who embraced the new ideas with all the enthusiasm of a lively imagination. He fancied liberty was to be secured by obtaining concessions from the king, whom he venerated. But all was lost, and nothing gained but anarchy. Who will arrest the torrent? O God! unless thy powerful hand control and restrain it, we are undone.

"For my part, my children, I am about to die, as your father died, a victim of the fury he always opposed, but to which he fell a sacrifice. I leave life without hatred of France and its assassins, whom I despise. But I am penetrated with sorrow for the misfortunes of my country. Honor my memory in sharing my sentiments. I leave for your inheritance the glory of your father and the name of your mother, whom some who have been unfortunate will bear in remembrance."

Chapter II
The Marriage of Josephine and General Bonaparte

The day before Josephine was to be led to her execution there was a new revolution in Paris. Robespierre and the party then in power were overthrown. From condemning others, they were condemned themselves. They had sent hundreds, in the cart of the executioner, to the guillotine. Now it was their turn to take that fatal ride, to ascend the steps of the scaffold, and to have their own heads severed by the keen edge of the knife. Those whom they had imprisoned were set at liberty.

As Josephine emerged from the gloom of her prison into the streets of Paris, she found herself a widow, homeless, almost friendless, and in the extreme of penury. But for her children, life would have been a burden from which she would have been glad to be relieved by the executioner's ax. The storms of revolution had dispersed all her friends, and terror reigned in Paris. Her children were living upon the charity of others. It was necessary to conceal their birth as the children of a noble, for the brutal threat of Marat ever rang in her ears, "We must exterminate all the whelps of aristocracy."

Hoping to conceal the illustrious lineage of Eugene and Hortense, and probably also impelled by the necessities of poverty, Josephine apprenticed her son to a house carpenter, and her daughter was placed, with other girls of more lowly birth, in the shop of a milliner. But Josephine's beauty of person, grace of manners, and culture of mind could not leave her long in obscurity. Everyone who met her was charmed with her unaffected loveliness. New friends were created, among them some who were in power. Through their interposition, a portion of her husband's confiscated estates was restored to her. She was thus provided with means of a frugal support for herself and her children. Engaging humble apartments, she devoted herself entirely to their education. Both of the children were richly endowed; inheriting from their mother and their father talents, personal loveliness, and an instinctive power of attraction.

Thus there came a brief lull in those dreadful storms of life by which Josephine had been so long buffeted.

But suddenly, like the transformations of the kaleidoscope, there came another and a marvelous change. All are familiar with the circumstances of her marriage to the young and rising general, Napoleon Bonaparte. This remarkable young man, enjoying the renown of having captured Toulon, and of having quelled a very formidable insurrection in the streets of Paris, was ordered by the then existing Government to disarm the whole Parisian population, that there might be no further attempt at insurrection. The officers who were sent, in performance of this duty, from house to house, took from Josephine the sword of her husband, which she had preserved as a sacred relic. The next day Eugene repaired to the headquarters of General Bonaparte to implore that the sword of his father might be restored to him. The young general was so much impressed with the grace and beauty of the boy, and with his artless and touching eloquence, that he made many inquiries respecting his parentage, treated him with marked tenderness, and promptly restored the sword. Josephine was so grateful for the kindness of General Bonaparte to Eugene, that the next day she drove to his quarters to express a mother's thanks. General Bonaparte was even more deeply impressed with the grace and loveliness of the mother than he had been with the child. He sought her acquaintance; this led to intimacy, to love, and to the proffer of marriage.

In the following letter to a friend Josephine expressed her views in reference to her marriage with General Bonaparte:

> "I am urged, my dear, to marry again by the advice of all my friends, and I may almost say, by the commands of my aunt and the prayers of my children. Why are you not here to help me by your advice, and to tell me whether I ought or not to consent to a union which certainly seems calculated to relieve me from the discomforts of my present situation? Your friendship would render you clear-sighted to my interests, and a word from you would suffice to bring me to a decision.
>
> "Among my visitors you have seen General Bonaparte. He is the man who wishes to become a father to the orphans of Alexander de Beauharnais, and husband to his widow.

Hortense

" 'Do you love him?' is naturally your first question. My answer is perhaps '*no*.' 'Do you dislike him?' 'No,' again. But the sentiments I entertain towards him are of that lukewarm kind which true devotees think worst of all, in matters of religion. Now love being a sort of religion, my feelings ought to be very different from what they really are. This is the point on which I want your advice, which would fix the wavering of my irresolute disposition. To come to a decision has always been too much for my Creole inertness, and I find it easier to obey the wishes of others.

"I admire the general's courage, the extent of his information on every subject on which he converses; his shrewd intelligence, which enables him to understand the thoughts of others before they are expressed. But I confess that I am somewhat fearful of that control which he seems anxious to exercise over all about him. There is something in his scrutinizing glance that cannot be described. It awes even our Directors. Therefore it may well be supposed to intimidate a woman. He talks of his passion for me with a degree of earnestness which renders it impossible to doubt his sincerity. Yet this very circumstance, which you would suppose likely to please me, is precisely that which has withheld me from giving the consent which I have often been upon the point of uttering.

"My spring of life is past. Can I then hope to preserve for any length of time that ardor of affection which in the general amounts almost to madness? If his love should cool, as it certainly will after our marriage, will he not reproach me for having prevented him from forming a more advantageous connection? What, then, shall I say? What shall I do? I may shut myself up and weep. Fine consolation truly, methinks I hear you say. But unavailing as I know it is, weeping is, I assure you, my only consolation whenever my poor heart receives a wound. Write to me quickly, and pray scold me if you think me wrong. You know everything is welcome that comes from you.

"Barras[1] assures me that if I marry the general, he will get him appointed commander-in-chief of the Army of Italy. This

---

[1]Barras, a leading member of the Directory, and a strong friend of General Bonaparte.

favor, though not yet granted, occasions some murmuring among Bonaparte's brother-officers. When speaking to me on the subject yesterday, General Bonaparte said:

" 'Do they think that I cannot get forward without their patronage? One day or other they will all be too happy if I grant them mine. I have a good sword by my side, which will carry me on.'

"What do you think of this self-confidence? Does it not savor of excessive vanity? A general of brigade to talk of patronizing the chiefs of Government? It is very ridiculous. Yet I know not how it happens, his ambitious spirit sometimes wins upon me so far that I am almost tempted to believe in the practicability of any project he takes into his head; and who can foresee what he may attempt?

"Madame Tallien desires me to present her love to you. She is still fair and good as ever. She employs her immense influence only for the benefit of the unfortunate. And when she performs a favor, she appears as pleased and satisfied as though she herself were the obliged party. Her friendship for me is most affectionate and sincere. And of my regard for her I need only say that it is equal to that which I entertain for you.

"Hortense grows more and more interesting every day. Her pretty figure is fully developed, and, if I were so inclined, I should have ample reason to rail at Time, who confers charms on the daughter at the expense of the mother. But truly I have other things to think of. I try to banish gloomy thoughts, and look forward to a more propitious future, for we shall soon meet, never to part again.

"But for this marriage, which harasses and unsettles me, I could be cheerful in spite of everything. Were it once over, happen what might, I could resign myself to my fate. I am inured to suffering, and, if I be destined to taste fresh sorrow, I can support it, provided my children, my aunt, and you remain to comfort me.

"You know we have agreed to dispense with all formal terminations to our letters. So adieu, my friend,

"JOSEPHINE."

In March, 1796, Josephine became the bride of Napoleon Bonaparte, then the most promising young general in France, and destined to become, in achievements and renown, the foremost man in all the world. Eugene was immediately taken into the service of his stepfather.

In the following letter to Eugene we have a pleasing revelation of the character of Hortense at that time, and of the affectionate relations existing between the mother and her children:

"I learn with pleasure, my dear Eugene, that your conduct is worthy of the name you bear, and of the protector under whom it is so easy to learn to become a great captain. Bonaparte has written to me that you are everything that he can wish. As he is no flatterer, my heart is proud to read your eulogy sketched by a hand which is usually far from being lavish in praise. You well know that I never doubted your capability to undertake great things, or the brilliant courage which you inherit. But you, alas! know how much I dislike your removal from me, fearing that your natural impetuosity might carry you too far, and that it might prevent you from submitting to the numerous petty details of discipline which must be very disagreeable when the rank is only subaltern.

"Judge, then, of my joy on learning that you remember my advice, and that you are as obedient to your superiors in command as you are kind and humane to those beneath you. This conduct, my child, makes me quite happy, and these words, I know, will reward you more than all the favors you can receive. Read them often, and repeat to yourself that your mother, though far from you, complains not of her lot, since she knows that yours will be brilliant, and will deserve so to be.

"Your sister shares all my feelings, and will tell you so herself. But that of which I am sure she will not speak, and which is therefore my duty to tell, is her attention to me and her aunt. Love her, my son, for to me she brings consolation, and she overflows with affection for you. She prosecutes her studies with uncommon success, but music, I think, will be the art she will carry to the highest perfection. With her sweet voice, which is now well cultivated, she sings romances in a manner that would surprise you. I have just bought her a new piano from the best maker, Erard, which redoubles her passion for that charming art which you prefer to every other. That perhaps accounts for your sister applying to it with so much assiduity.

"Were you here, you would be telling me a thousand times a day to beware of the men who pay particular attention to Hortense. Some there are who do so whom you do not like, and whom you seem to fear she may prefer. Set your mind at rest. She is a bit of a coquette, is pleased with her success, and torments her victims, but her heart is free. I am the confidante of all her thoughts and feelings, which have hitherto been just what they ought to be. She now knows that when she thinks of marrying, it is not my consent alone she has to seek, and that my will is subordinate to that of the man to whom we owe everything. The knowledge of this fact must prevent her from fixing her choice in a way that may not meet the approval of Bonaparte, and the latter will not give your sister in marriage to anyone to whom you can object."

There was now an end to poverty and obscurity. The rise of Napoleon was so brilliant and rapid that Josephine was speedily placed at the head of society in Paris, and vast crowds were eager to do her homage. Never before did man move with strides so rapid. The lapse of a few months transformed her from almost a homeless, friendless, impoverished widow, to be the bride of one whose advancing greatness seemed to outvie the wildest creations of fiction. The unsurpassed splendor of Napoleon's achievements crowded the saloons of Josephine with statesmen, philosophers, generals, and all who ever hasten to the shrine of rising greatness.

After the campaign of Italy, which gave Napoleon not only a French but a European reputation for military genius and diplomatic skill, he took command of the Army of Egypt. Josephine accompanied him to Toulon. Standing upon a balcony, she with tearful eyes watched the receding fleet which bore her husband to that far-distant land, until it disappeared beneath the horizon of the blue Mediterranean. Eugene accompanied his father. Hortense remained with her mother, who took up her residence most of the time during her husband's absence at Plombières, a celebrated watering-place.

Josephine, anxious in every possible way to promote the popularity of her absent husband, and thus to secure his advancement, received with cordiality all who came to her with their congratulations. She was endowed with marvelous power of pleasing. Everyone who saw her was charmed with her. Hortense was bewitchingly beautiful and attractive.

Josephine had ample means to indulge her taste in entertainments, and was qualified eminently to shine in such scenes. The consequence was that her saloons were the constant resort of rank and wealth and fashion. Some enemy wrote to Napoleon, and roused his jealousy to a very high degree, by representing Josephine as forgetting her husband, immersed in pleasure, and coquetting with all the world.

Napoleon was exceedingly disturbed, and wrote Josephine a very severe letter. The following extract from her reply fully explains the nature of this momentary estrangement:

> "Is it possible, general, that the letter I have just received comes from you? I can scarcely credit it when I compare that letter with others to which your love imparts so many charms. My eyes, indeed, would persuade me that your hands traced these lines, but my heart refuses to believe that a letter from you could ever have caused the mortal anguish I experience on perusing these expressions of your displeasure, which afflict me the more when I consider how much pain they must have caused you.
>
> "I know not what I have done to provoke some malignant enemy to destroy my peace by disturbing yours. But certainly a powerful motive must influence someone in continually renewing calumnies against me, and giving them a sufficient appearance of probability to impose on the man who has hitherto judged me worthy of his affection and confidence. These two sentiments are necessary to my happiness. And if they are to be so soon withdrawn from me, I can only regret that I was ever blest in possessing them or knowing you.
>
> "On my first acquaintance with you, the affliction with which I was overwhelmed led me to believe that my heart must ever remain a stranger to any sentiment resembling love. The sanguinary scenes of which I had been a witness and a victim constantly haunted my thoughts. I therefore apprehended no danger to myself from the frequent

enjoyment of your society. Still less did I imagine that I could for a single moment fix your choice.

"I, like everyone else, admired your talents and acquirements. And better than anyone else I foresaw your future glory. But still I loved you only for the services you rendered to my country. Why did you seek to convert admiration into a more tender sentiment, by availing yourself of all those powers of pleasing with which you are so eminently gifted, since, so shortly after having united your destiny with mine, you regret the felicity you have conferred upon me?

"Do you think I can ever forget the love with which you once cherished me? Can I ever become indifferent to the man who has blest me with the most enthusiastic and ardent passion? Can I ever efface from my memory your paternal affection for Hortense, the advice and example you have given Eugene? If all this appears impossible, how can you, for a moment, suspect me of bestowing a thought upon any but yourself?

"Instead of listening to traducers, who, for reasons which I cannot explain, seek to disturb our happiness, why do you not silence them by enumerating the benefits you have bestowed on a woman whose heart could never be reached with ingratitude? The knowledge of what you have done for my children would check the malignity of these calumniators; for they would then see that the strongest link of my attachment for you depends on my character as a mother. Your subsequent conduct, which has claimed the admiration of all Europe, could have no other effect than to make me adore the husband who gave me his hand when I was poor and unfortunate. Every step you take adds to the glory of the name I bear. Yet this is the moment which has been selected for persuading you that I no longer love you! Surely nothing can be more wicked and absurd than the conduct of those who are about you, and are jealous of your marked superiority.

"Yes, I still love you, and no less tenderly than ever. Those who allege the contrary know that they speak falsely. To those very persons I have frequently written to inquire about you, and to recommend them to console you, by their friendship, for the absence of her who is your best and truest friend.

"I acknowledge that I see a great deal of company; for everyone is eager to compliment me on your success, and I confess that I have not resolution to close my door against those who speak of you. I also confess that a great portion of my visitors are gentlemen. Men understand your bold projects better than women; and they speak with enthusiasm of your glorious achievements, while my female friends only complain of you for having carried away their husbands, brothers, or fathers.

"I take no pleasure in their society if they do not praise you. Yet there are some among them whose hearts and understandings claim my highest regard, because they entertain sincere friendship for you. In this number I may mention ladies Arquillon, Tallien, and my aunt. They are almost constantly with me; and they can tell you, ungrateful as you are, whether *I have been coquetting with everybody.* These are your words. And they would be hateful to me were I not certain that you had disavowed them, and are sorry for having written them.

"I sometimes receive honors here which cause me no small degree of embarrassment. I am not accustomed to this sort of homage. And I see that it is displeasing to our authorities, who are always suspicious and fearful of losing their newly-gotten power. If they are envious now, what will they be when you return crowned with fresh laurels? Heaven knows to what lengths their malignity will then carry them. But you will be here, and then nothing can vex me.

"But I will say no more of them, nor of your suspicions, which I do not refute one by one, because they are all equally devoid of probability. And to make amends for the unpleasant commencement of this letter, I will tell you something which I know will please you.

"Hortense, in her efforts to console me, endeavors as far as possible to conceal her anxiety for you and her brother. And she exerts all her ingenuity to banish that melancholy, the existence of which you doubt, but which I assure you never forsakes me. If by her lively conversation and interesting talents she sometimes succeeds in drawing a smile, she joyfully exclaims, 'Dear mamma, that will be known at Cairo.' The fatal word immediately calls to my mind the distance which separates me from you and my son, and restores the melancholy which it was intended to divert. I am obliged to make great efforts to conceal my grief from my daughter, who, by a word or a look, transports me to the very place which she would wish to banish from my thoughts.

"Hortense's figure is daily becoming more and more graceful. She dresses with great taste; and though not quite so handsome as your sisters, she may certainly be thought agreeable when even they are present.

"Heaven knows when or where you may receive this letter. May it restore you to that confidence which you ought never to have lost, and convince you, more than ever, that, long as I live, I shall love you as dearly as I did on the day of our separation. Adieu. Believe me, love me, and receive a thousand kisses.

"Josephine."

There was at that time a very celebrated female school at St. Germain, under the care of Madame Campan. This illustrious lady was familiar with all the etiquette of the court, and was also endowed with a superior mind highly cultivated. At the early age of fifteen she had been appointed reader to the daughter of Louis XV. Maria Antoinette took a strong fancy to her, and made her a friend and companion. The crumbling of the throne of the Bourbons and the dispersion of the court left Madame Campan without a home, and caused what the world would call her ruin.

But in the view of true intelligence this reverse of fortune only elevated her to a far higher position of responsibility, usefulness, and power. Impelled by necessity, she opened a boarding school for young ladies at St. Germain. The school soon acquired celebrity. Almost every illustrious family in France sought to place their daughters under her care. She thus educated very many young ladies who subsequently occupied very important positions in society as the wives and mothers of distinguished men. Some of her pupils attained to royalty. Thus the boarding school of Madame Campan became a great power in France.

Hortense was sent to this school with Napoleon's sister Caroline, who subsequently became Queen of Naples, and with Stephanie Beauharnais, to whom we shall have occasion hereafter to refer as Duchess of Baden. Stephanie was a cousin of Hortense, being a daughter of her father's brother, the Marquis de Beauharnais.

In this school Hortense formed many very strong attachments. Her most intimate friend, however, whom she loved with affection which never waned, was a niece of Madame Campan, by the name of Adèle Auguié, afterwards Madame de Broc, whose sad fate, hereafter to be described, was one of the heaviest blows which fell upon Hortense. It would seem that Hortense was not at all injured by the flattery lavished upon her in consequence of the renown of her father. She retained, unchanged, all her native simplicity of character, which she had inherited from her mother, and which she ever saw illustrated in her mother's words and actions. Treating the humblest with the same kindness as the most exalted, she won all hearts, and made herself the friend of everyone in the school.

But her cousin Stephanie was a very different character. Her father, the Marquis, had fled from France an emigrant. He was an aristocrat by birth, and in all his cherished sentiments. In his flight with the nobles, from the terrors of the revolution, he had left his daughter behind, as the protégée of Josephine. Inheriting a haughty disposition, and elated by the grandeur which her uncle was attaining, she assumed consequential airs which rendered her disagreeable to many of her companions. The eagle eye of Josephine detected these faults in the character of her niece. As Stephanie returned to school from one of her vacations, Josephine sent by her the following letter to Madame Campan:

"In returning to you my niece, my dear Madame Campan, I send you both thanks and reproof:—thanks for the brilliant education you have given her, and reproof for the faults which your acuteness must have noticed, but which your indulgence has passed over. She is good-tempered, but cold; well-informed, but disdainful; lively, but deficient in judgment. She pleases no one, and it gives her no pain. She fancies the renown of her uncle and the gallantry of her father are everything. Teach her, but teach her plainly, without mincing, that in reality they are nothing.

"We live in an age when everyone is the child of his own deeds. And if they who fill the highest ranks of public service enjoy any superior advantage or privilege, it is the opportunity to be more useful and more beloved. It is thus alone that good fortune becomes pardonable in the eyes of the envious. This is what I would have you repeat to her constantly. I wish her to treat all her companions as her equals. Many of them are better, or at least quite as deserving as she is herself, and their only inferiority is in not having had relations equally skillful or equally fortunate.

"Josephine Bonaparte."

On the 8th of October, 1799, Napoleon landed at Fréjus, on his return from Egypt. His mind was still very much disturbed with the reports which had reached him respecting Josephine. Fréjus was six hundred miles from Paris—a long journey, when railroads were unknown. The intelligence of his arrival was promptly communicated to the metropolis by telegraph. Josephine received the news at midnight. Without an hour's delay she entered her carriage with Hortense, taking as a protector Napoleon's younger brother Louis, who subsequently married Hortense, and set out to meet her husband. Almost at the same hour Napoleon left Fréjus for Paris.

When Josephine reached Lyons, a distance of two hundred and forty-two miles from Paris, she learned, to her consternation, that Napoleon had left the city several hours before her arrival, and that they had passed each other by different roads. Her anguish was dreadful. For many months she had not received a line from her husband, as all communication had been intercepted by the British cruisers. She knew that her enemies would be busy in poisoning the mind of her husband against her. She had traversed the weary leagues of her journey without a moment's intermission, and now, faint, exhausted, and despairing, she was to retrace her steps, to reach Paris only many hours after Napoleon would have arrived there. Probably in all France there was not then a more unhappy woman than Josephine.

The mystery of human love and jealousy no philosophy can explain. Secret wretchedness was gnawing at the heart of Napoleon. He loved Josephine with intensest passion, and all the pride of his nature was roused by the conviction that she had trifled with him. With these conflicting emotions rending his soul, he entered Paris and drove to his dwelling. Josephine was not there. Even Josephine had bitter enemies, as all who are in power ever must have. These enemies took advantage of her absence to fan the flames of that jealousy which Napoleon could not conceal. It was represented to him that Josephine had fled from her home, afraid to meet the anger of her injured husband. As he paced the floor in anguish, which led him to forget all his achievements in the past and all his hopes for the future, an enemy maliciously remarked,

"Josephine will soon appear before you with all her arts of fascination. She will explain matters, you will forgive all, and tranquility will be restored."

Napoleon, striding nervously up and down the floor, replied with pallid cheek and trembling lip,

"Never! never! Were I not sure of my resolution, I would tear out this heart and cast it into the fire."

Eugene had returned with Napoleon. He loved his mother to adoration. Anxiously he sat at the window watching, hour after hour, for her arrival. At midnight on the 19th the rattle of her carriage-wheels was heard, as she entered the courtyard of their dwelling in the Rue Chantereine. Eugene rushed to his mother's arms. Napoleon had ever been the most courteous of husbands. Whenever Josephine returned, even from an ordinary morning drive, he would leave any engagements to greet her as she alighted from her carriage. But now, after an absence of eighteen months, he remained sternly in his chamber, the victim of almost unearthly misery.

In a state of terrible agitation, with limbs tottering and heart throbbing, Josephine, assisted by Eugene and accompanied by Hortense, ascended the stairs to the parlor where she had so often received the caresses of her husband. She opened the door. Napoleon stood before her, pale, motionless as a marble statue. Without one kind word of greeting he said sternly, in words which pierced her heart, "Madame, it is my wish that you retire immediately to Malmaison."

The meek and loving Josephine uttered not a word. She would have fallen senseless to the floor, had she not been caught in the arms of her son. It was midnight. For a week she had lived in her carriage almost without sleep. She was in a state of utter exhaustion, both of body and of mind. It was twelve miles to Malmaison. Napoleon had

The reconciliation.

Hortense

no idea that she would leave the house until the morning. Much to his surprise, he soon heard the carriage in the yard, and Josephine, accompanied by Eugene and Hortense, descending the stairs. The naturally kind heart of Napoleon could not assent to such cruelty. Immediately going down into the yard, though his pride would not permit him to speak to Josephine, he addressed Eugene, and requested them all to return for refreshment and repose.

In silent submission, Eugene and Hortense conducted their mother to her apartment, where she threw herself upon her couch in abject misery. In equally sleepless woe, Napoleon retired to his cabinet. Two days of wretchedness passed away. On the third, the love for Josephine, which still reigned in the heart of Napoleon, so far triumphed that he entered her apartment. Josephine was seated at a toilette-table, with her head bowed, and her eyes buried in her handkerchief. The table was covered with the letters which she had received from Napoleon, and which she had evidently been perusing. Hortense, the victim of grief and despair, was standing in the alcove of a window.

Apparently Josephine did not hear the approaching footsteps of her husband. He advanced softly to her chair, placed his hand upon it, and said, in tones almost of wonted kindness, "Josephine." She started at the sound of that well-known and dearly-loved voice, and turning towards him her swollen and flooded eyes, responded, "My dear." The words of tenderness, the loving voice, brought back with resistless rush the memory of the past. Napoleon was vanquished. He extended his hand to Josephine. She rose, threw her arms around his neck, rested her throbbing, aching head upon his bosom, and wept in convulsions of anguish. A long explanation ensued. Napoleon again pressed Josephine to his loving heart, satisfied, perfectly satisfied that he had deeply wronged her; that she had been the victim of base traducers. The reconciliation was perfect.

Soon after this Napoleon overthrew the Directory, and established the Consulate. This was on the ninth of November, 1799, usually called 18th Brumaire. Napoleon was thirty years of age, and was now First Consul of France. After the wonderful achievements of this day of peril, during which Napoleon had not been able to send a single line to his wife, at four o'clock in the morning he alighted from his carriage at the door of his dwelling at the Rue Chantereine. Josephine, in a state of great anxiety, was watching at the window for his approach.

She sprang to meet him. Napoleon encircled her in his arms, and briefly recapitulated the memorable scenes of the day. He assured her that since he had taken the oath of office, he had not allowed himself to speak to a single individual, for he wished the beloved voice of his Josephine might be the first to congratulate him upon his virtual accession to the Empire of France. Throwing himself upon a couch for a few moments of repose, he exclaimed gaily, "Good-night, my Josephine. Tomorrow we sleep in the palace of the Luxembourg."

This renowned palace, with its vast saloons, its galleries of art, its garden, is one of the most attractive of residences. Napoleon was now virtually the monarch of France. Josephine was a queen, Eugene and Hortense prince and princess. Strange must have been the emotions of Josephine and her children as, encompassed with regal splendor, they took up their residence in the palace. But a few years before, Josephine, in poverty, friendlessness, and intensest anguish of heart, had led her children by the hand through those halls to visit her imprisoned husband. From one of those apartments the husband and father had been led to his trial, and to the scaffold, and now this mother enters this palace virtually a queen, and her children have opening before them the very highest positions of earthly wealth and honor.

Chapter III
Hortense and Duroc

It is a very unamiable trait in human nature, that many persons are more eager to believe that which is bad in the character of others than that which is good. The same voice of calumny, which has so mercilessly assailed Josephine, has also traduced Hortense. It is painful to witness the readiness with which even now the vilest slanders, devoid of all evidence, can be heaped upon a noble and virtuous woman who is in her grave.

In the days of Napoleon's power, he himself, his mother, his wife, his sisters, and his stepdaughter, Hortense, were assailed with the most envenomed accusations malice could engender. These infamous assaults, which generally originated with the British Tory press, still have lingering echoes throughout the world. There are those who seem to consider it no crime to utter the most atrocious accusations, even without a shadow of proof, against those who are not living. Well do the "Berkeley men" say:

"The Bonapartes, especially the women of that family, have always been too proud and haughty to degrade themselves. Even had they lacked what is technically called moral character, their virtue has been entrenched behind their ancestry, and the achievements of their own family. Nor was there at any time an instant when any one of the Bonapartes could have overstepped, by a hair's-breadth, the line of decency, without being fatally exposed. None of them pursued the noiseless tenor of their way along the vale of obscurity. They were walking in the clear sunshine, on the topmost summits of the earth, and millions of enemies were watching every step they took. The highest genius of historians, the bitterest satire of dramatists, the meanest and most malignant pen of the journalists have assailed them for half a century. We have written these words because a Republican is the only man likely to speak well of the Bonaparte family. It was, and is, and will be the dynasty of the people, standing there from 1804, a fearful antagonism against the feudal age and its souvenirs of oppression and crime."

Napoleon at St. Helena said: "Of all the libels and pamphlets with which the English ministers have inundated Europe, there is not one which will reach posterity. When there shall not be a trace of those libels to be found, the great monuments of utility which I have reared, and the code of laws which I have formed, will descend to the remotest ages; and future historians will avenge the wrongs done me by my contemporaries. There was a time when all crimes seemed to belong to me of right. Thus I poisoned Hoche, strangled Pichegru in his cell, I caused Kleber to be assassinated in Egypt, I blew out Desaix's brains at Marengo, I cut the throats of persons who were confined in prison, I dragged the Pope by the hair of his head, and a hundred similar abominations. And yet I have not seen one of those libels which is worthy of an answer. These are so contemptible and so absurdly false, that they do not merit any other notice than to write *false, false,* on every page."

It is well known, by everyone acquainted with the past history of our country, that George Washington was assailed in the severest possible language of vituperation. He was charged with military inability, administrative incapacity, mental weakness, and gross personal immorality. He was denounced as a murderer, and a hoary-headed traitor. This is the doom of those in power. And thousands of men in those days believed those charges.

It is seldom possible to prove a negative. But no evidence has ever been brought forward to substantiate the rumors brought against Hortense. These vile slanderers have even gone so far as to accuse Napoleon of crimes, in reference to the daughter of Josephine and the wife of his brother, which, if true, should consign him to eternal infamy. The "Berkeley men," after making the most thorough historic investigations in writing the life both of Louis Bonaparte and Hortense, say:

"Louis was a little over twenty-three years of age at the time of his marriage. Hortense was nineteen. In his memoirs Louis treats with scorn and contempt the absurd libels respecting his domestic affairs, involving the purity of his wife's character and the legitimacy of his children. Napoleon, also, in his conversations at St. Helena, thought proper to allude to the subject, and indignantly to repel the charges which had been made against Hortense, at the same time showing the entire improbability of the stories about her and her offspring. *We have found nothing, in our investigations on this subject to justify even a suspicion against the morals or integrity of Louis or Hortense; and we here dismiss the subject with the remark that, there is more cause for sympathy with the parties to this unhappy union than of censure for their conduct."*

The Duchess of Abrantes, who was intimately acquainted with Hortense from her childhood and with the whole Bonaparte family, in her interesting memoirs writes: "Hortense de Beauharnais was fresh as a rose; and though her fair complexion was not relieved by much color, she had enough to produce that freshness and bloom which was her chief beauty. A profusion of light hair played in silky locks round her soft and penetrating blue eyes. The delicate roundness of her slender figure was set off by the elegant carriage of her head. Her feet were small and pretty, her hands very white, with pink, well-rounded nails. But what formed the chief attraction of Hortense was the grace and suavity of her manners. She was gay, gentle, amiable. She had wit which, without the smallest ill-temper, had just malice enough to be amusing. A polished education had improved her natural talents. She drew excellently, sang harmoniously, and performed admirably in comedy. In 1800 she was a charming young girl. She afterwards became one of the most amiable princesses in Europe. I have seen many, both in their own courts and in Paris, but I have never known one who had any pretensions to equal talents. Her brother loved her tenderly. The First Consul looked upon her as his child. And it is only in that country so fertile in the inventions of scandal, that so foolish an accusation could have been imagined, as that any feeling less pure than paternal affection actuated his conduct towards her. The vile calumny met the contempt it merited."

The testimony of Bourrienne upon this point is decisive. Bourrienne had been the private secretary of Napoleon, had become his enemy, and had joined the Bourbons. Upon the downfall of the Emperor he wrote a very hostile life of Napoleon, being then in the employment of the Bourbons. In those envenomed pages, Bourrienne says that he has written severely enough against Napoleon, to have his word believed when he makes any admission in his favor. He then writes:

"Napoleon never cherished for Hortense any feeling but a real paternal tenderness. He loved her, after his marriage with her mother, as he would have loved his own child. For three years at least I was witness to all their most private actions. I declare that I never saw anything which could furnish the least ground for suspicion or the slightest trace of culpable intimacy. This calumny must be classed with those which malice delights to take with the character of men who become celebrated; calumnies which are adopted lightly and without reflection.

"I freely declare that, did I retain the slightest doubt with regard to this odious charge, I would avow it. But it is not true. Napoleon is no more. Let his memory be accompanied only by that, be it good or bad, which really took place. Let not this complaint be made against him by the impartial historian. I must say, in conclusion, on this delicate subject, that Napoleon's principles were rigid in the extreme; and that any fault of the nature charged neither entered his mind, nor was in accordance with his morals or taste."

Notwithstanding this abundant testimony, and notwithstanding the fact that no contradictory testimony can be adduced, which any historian could be pardoned for treating with respect, there are still men to be found who will repeat those foul slanders, which ought long since to have died away.

Napoleon remained but two months in the palace of the Luxembourg. In the meantime the palace of the Tuileries, which had been sacked by revolutionary mobs, was re-furnished with much splendor. In February the Court of the Consuls was transferred to the Tuileries. Napoleon had so entirely eclipsed his colleagues that he alone was thought of by the Parisian populace. The royal apartments were prepared for Napoleon. The more humble apartments, in the Pavilion of Flora, were assigned to the two other consuls. The transfer from the Luxembourg was made with great pomp, in one of those brilliant parades which ever delight the eyes of the Parisians. Six thousand picked soldiers, with a gorgeous train of officers, formed his escort. Twenty thousand troops with all the concomitants of military parade, lined the streets. A throng, from city and country, which could not be numbered, gazed upon the scene. Napoleon took his seat in a magnificent carriage drawn by six beautiful white horses. The suite of rooms assigned to Josephine consisted of two large parlors furnished with regal splendor, and several adjoining private rooms. Here Hortense, a beautiful girl of about eighteen, found herself at home in the apartments of the ancient kings of France.

In the evening a brilliant assembly was gathered in the saloons of Josephine. As she entered, with queenly grace, leaning upon the arm of Talleyrand, a murmur of admiration rose from the whole multitude. She wore a robe of white muslin. Her hair fell in ringlets upon her neck and shoulders, through which gleamed a necklace of priceless pearls. The festivities were protracted until a late hour in the morning. It was said that Josephine gained a social victory that evening, corresponding with that which Napoleon had gained in the pageant of the day. In these scenes Hortense shone with great brilliance. She was young, beautiful, graceful, amiable, witty, and very highly accomplished. In addition to this, she was the stepdaughter of the First Consul, who was ascending in a career of grandeur which was to terminate no one could tell where.

During Napoleon's absence in Egypt Josephine had purchased the beautiful estate of Malmaison. This was their favorite home. The chateau was a very convenient, attractive, but not very spacious rural edifice, surrounded with extensive grounds, ornamented with lawns, shrubbery, and forest-trees. With the Tuileries for her city residence, Malmaison for her rural retreat, Napoleon for her father, Josephine for her mother, Eugene for her brother; with the richest endowments of person, mind, and heart, with glowing health, and surrounded by admirers, Hortense seemed now to be placed upon the very highest pinnacle of earthly happiness.

Josephine and Hortense resided at Malmaison when Napoleon made his ten months' campaign into Italy, which was terminated by the victory of Marengo. They both busily employed their time in making those improvements on the place which would create a pleasant surprise for Napoleon on his return. Here they opened a new path through the forest; here they spanned a stream with a beautiful rustic bridge; upon a gentle eminence a pavilion rose; and new parterres of flowers gladdened the eye. Every charm was thrown around the place which the genius and taste of Josephine and Hortense could suggest. At midnight, on the second of July, Napoleon returned to Paris, and immediately hastened to the arms of his wife and daughter at Malmaison. He was so pleased with its retirement and rural beauty that, forgetting the splendors of Fontainebleau and Saint Cloud, he ever after made it his favorite residence. Fortunate is the tourist who can obtain permission to saunter through those lovely walks, where the father, the wife, and the daughter, for a few brief months, walked almost daily, arm in arm, in the enjoyment of nearly all the happiness which they were destined on earth to share.

The Emperor, at the close of his career, said upon his dying bed at St. Helena,

"I am indebted for all the little happiness I have enjoyed on earth to the love of Josephine."

Hortense and her mother frequently rode on horseback, both being very graceful riders, and very fond of that recreation. At moments when Napoleon could unbend from the cares of state, the family amused themselves, with such guests as were present, in the game of "prisoners" on the lawn. For several years this continued to be the favorite pastime at Malmaison. Kings and queens were often seen among the pursuers and the pursued on the green sward.

It was observed that Napoleon was always solicitous to have Josephine on his side. And whenever, in the progress of the game, she was taken prisoner, he was nervously anxious until she was rescued. Napoleon, who had almost lived upon horseback, was a poor runner, and would often, in his eagerness, fall, rolling headlong over the grass, raising shouts of laughter. Josephine and Hortense were as agile as they were graceful.

On the 24th of December, 1800, Napoleon, Josephine, and Hortense were going to the opera, to hear Haydn's Oratorio of the Creation. It was then to be performed for the first time. Napoleon, busily engaged in business, went reluctantly at the earnest solicitation of Josephine. Three gentlemen rode with Napoleon in his carriage. Josephine, with Hortense and other friends, followed in her private carriage. As the carriages were passing through the narrow street of St. Nicaire, a tremendous explosion took place, which was heard all over Paris. An infernal machine, of immense power, had been conveyed to the spot, concealed beneath a cart, which was intended, at whatever sacrifice of the lives of others, to render the assassination of the First Consul certain. Eight persons were instantly killed; more than sixty were wounded. Several buildings were nearly demolished. The windows of both carriages were dashed in, and the shattered vehicles were tossed to and fro like ships in a storm. Napoleon almost miraculously escaped unharmed. Hortense was slightly wounded by the broken glass. Still they all heroically went on to the opera, where, in view of their providential escape, they were received with thunders of applause.

It was at first supposed that the Jacobins were the authors of this infamous plot. It was afterwards proved to be a conspiracy of the

Royalists. Josephine, whose husband had bled beneath the slide of the guillotine, and who had narrowly escaped the ax herself, with characteristic humanity forgot the peril to which she and her friends had been exposed, in sympathy for those who were to suffer for the crime. The criminals were numerous. They were the nobles with whom Josephine had formerly lived in terms of closest intimacy. She wrote to Fouché, the Minister of Police, in behalf of these families about to be plunged into woe by the merited punishment of the conspirators. This letter reflects such light upon the character of Josephine, which character she transmitted to Hortense, that it claims insertion here.

"Citizen Minister,—While I yet tremble at the frightful event which has just occurred, I am disquieted and distressed through fear of the punishment necessarily to be inflicted on the guilty, who belong, it is said, to families with whom I once lived in habits of intercourse. I shall be solicited by mothers, sisters, and disconsolate wives, and my heart will be broken through my inability to obtain all the mercy for which I would plead.

"I know that the clemency of the First Consul is great; his attachment to me extreme. But the crime is too dreadful that a terrible example should not be necessary. The chief of the Government has not been alone exposed. It is that which will render him severe, inflexible. I conjure you, therefore, to do all in your power to prevent inquiries being pushed too far. Do not detect all those persons who may have been accomplices in these odious transactions. Let not France, so long overwhelmed in consternation by public executions, groan anew beneath such inflictions. It is even better to endeavor to soothe the public mind than to exasperate men by fresh terrors. In short, when the ringleaders of this nefarious attempt shall have been secured, let severity give place to pity for inferior agents, seduced, as they may have been, by dangerous falsehoods or exaggerated opinions.

"When just invested with supreme power, the First Consul, as seems to me, ought rather to gain hearts, than to be exhibited as ruling slaves. Soften by your counsels whatever may be too violent in his just resentment. Punish—alas! that you must certainly do—but pardon still more. Be also the support of those unfortunate men who, by frank avowal or repentance, shall expiate a portion of their crime.

"Having myself narrowly escaped perishing in the Revolution, you must regard as quite natural my interference on behalf of those who can be saved without involving in new danger the life of my husband, precious to me and to France. On this account do, I entreat you, make a wide distinction between the authors of the crime and those who, through weakness or fear, have consented to take part therein. As a woman, a wife, a mother, I must feel the heart-rendings of those who will apply to me. Act, citizen minister, in such a manner that the number of these may be lessened. This will spare me much grief. Never will I turn away from the supplications of misfortune. But in the present instance you can do infinitely more than I, and you will, on this account, excuse my importunity. Rely on my gratitude and esteem."

There was a young officer about twenty-nine years of age, by the name of Michel Duroc, who was then a frequent visitor at the Tuileries and Malmaison. He was a great favorite of Napoleon, and was distinguished alike for beauty of person and gallantry upon the field of battle. Born of an ancient family, young Duroc, having received a thorough military education, attached himself, with enthusiastic devotion, to the fortunes of Napoleon. He attracted the attention of General Bonaparte during his first Italian campaign, where he was appointed one of his aides. Following Napoleon to Egypt, he gained renown in many battles, and was speedily promoted to the rank of chief of battalion, and then to general of brigade. At Jaffa he performed a deed of gallantry, which was rewarded by the applauding shouts of nearly the whole army. At Jean d'Acre he led one of the most bloody and obstinate assaults recorded in the military annals of France, where he was severely wounded by the bursting of a howitzer. At the battle of Aboukir he won great applause. Napoleon's attachment to this young officer was such, that he took him to Paris on his return from Egypt. In the eventful day of the 18th Brumaire, Duroc stood by the side of Napoleon, and rendered him eminent service. The subsequent career of this very noble young man brilliantly reflects his worth and character. Rapidly rising, he became grand marshal of the palace and Duke of Friuli.

The memorable career of General Duroc was terminated at the battle of Bautzen, in Germany, on the 23d of May, 1813. He was struck by the last ball thrown from the batteries of the enemy. The affecting scene of his death was as follows:

"In the early dawn of the morning of the 23d of May, Napoleon was on horseback directing the movements of his troops against the routed foe. He soon overtook the rear-guard of the enemy, which had strongly posted its batteries on an eminence to protect the retreat of the discomfited army. A brief but fierce conflict ensued, and one of Napoleon's aides was struck dead at his feet. Duroc was riding by the side of the Emperor. Napoleon turned to him and said, 'Duroc, fortune is determined to have one of us today.' Hour after hour the incessant battle raged, as the advance-guard of the Emperor drove before it the rear-guard of the Allies. In the afternoon, as the Emperor, with a portion of the Imperial Guard, four abreast, was passing through a ravine, enveloped in a blinding cloud of dust and smoke, a cannon-ball, glancing from a tree, killed one officer, and mortally wounded Duroc, tearing out his entrails. The tumult and obscurity were such that Napoleon did not witness the casualty. When informed of it, he seemed for a moment overwhelmed with grief, and then exclaimed, in faltering accents,

"Duroc! gracious Heaven, my presentiments never deceive me. This is a sad day, a fatal day."

Immediately alighting from his horse, he walked to and fro for a short time absorbed in painful thoughts, while the thunders of the battle resounded unheeded around him. Then turning to Caulaincourt, he said,

"Alas! when will fate relent? When will there be an end of this? My eagles will yet triumph, but the happiness which accompanies them is fled. Whither has he been conveyed? I must see him. Poor, poor Duroc!"

The Emperor found the dying marshal in a cottage, still stretched upon the camp litter by which he had been conveyed from the field. Pallid as marble from the loss of blood, and with features distorted with agony, he was scarcely recognizable. The Emperor approached the litter, threw his arms around the neck of the friend he so tenderly loved, and exclaimed, in tones of deepest grief, "Alas! then is there no hope?"

"None whatever," the physicians replied.

The dying man took the hand of Napoleon, and gazing upon him affectionately, said, "Sire, my whole life has been devoted to your service, and now my only regret is that I can no longer be useful to you." Napoleon, in a voice almost inarticulate with emotion, said,

"Duroc, there is another life. There you will await me."

"Yes, sire," the marshal faintly replied, "but that will be thirty years hence. You will then have triumphed over your enemies, and realized the hopes of our country. I have lived an honest man. I have nothing to reproach myself with. I have a daughter, to whom your Majesty will be a father."

Napoleon was so deeply affected that he remained for some time in silence, incapable of uttering a word, but still affectionately holding the hand of his dying friend.

Duroc was the first to break the silence. "Sire," he said, "this sight pains you. Leave me."

The Emperor pressed his hand to his lips, embraced him affectionately, and saying sadly, "Adieu, my friend," hurried out of the room.

Supported by Marshal Soult and Caulaincourt, Napoleon, overwhelmed with grief, retired to his tent, which had been immediately pitched in the vicinity of the cottage. "This is horrible," he exclaimed. "My excellent, my dear Duroc! Oh, what a loss is this!"

His eyes were flooded with tears, and for the moment, forgetting everything but his grief, he retired to the solitude of his inner tent.

The squares of the Old Guard, sympathizing in the anguish of their commander and their sovereign, silently encamped around him. Napoleon sat alone in his tent, wrapped in his gray greatcoat, his forehead resting upon his hand, absorbed in painful musings. For some time none of his officers were willing to intrude upon his grief. At length two of the generals ventured to consult him respecting arrangements which it seemed necessary to make for the following day. Napoleon shook his head and replied, "Ask me nothing till tomorrow," and again covering his eyes with his hand, he resumed his attitude of meditation. Night came. One by one the stars came out. The moon rose brilliantly in the cloudless sky. The soldiers moved with noiseless footsteps, and spoke in subdued tones. The rumbling of wagons and the occasional boom of a distant gun alone disturbed the stillness of the scene.

"Those brave soldiers," says J. T. Headley, "filled with grief to see their beloved chief bowed down by such sorrows, stood for a long time silent and tearful. At length, to break the mournful silence, and to express the sympathy they might not speak, the band struck up a requiem for the dying marshal. The melancholy strains arose and fell in prolonged echoes over the field, and swept in softened cadences on the ear of the fainting, dying warrior. But still Napoleon moved not. They changed the measure to a triumphant strain, and the thrilling trumpets breathed forth their most joyful notes till the heavens rang with the melody. Such bursts of music welcomed Napoleon as he returned, flushed with victory, till his eye kindled with exultation. But now they fell on a dull and listless ear. It ceased, and again the mournful requiem filled all the air. But nothing could rouse him from his agonizing reflections. His friend lay dying, and the heart that he loved more than his life was throbbing its last pulsations. What a theme for a painter, and what a eulogy was that scene! That noble heart, which the enmity of the world could not shake, nor the terrors of the battlefield move from its calm repose, nor even the hatred nor the insults of his at last victorious enemies humble, here sank in the moment of victory before the tide of affection. What military chieftain ever mourned thus on the field of victory, and what soldiers ever loved their leader so!"

Before the dawn of the morning Duroc expired. When the event was announced to Napoleon, he said sadly, "All is over. He is released from his misery. Well, he is happier than I." The Emperor ordered a monument to be reared to his memory, and, when afterwards dying at St. Helena, left to the daughter of Duroc one of the largest legacies bequeathed in his will. That Duroc was worthy of this warm affection of the Emperor, may be inferred from the following testimony of Caulaincourt, Duke of Vicenza:

"Marshal Duroc was one of those men who seem too pure and perfect for this world, and whose excellence helps to reconcile us to human nature. In the high station to which the Emperor had wisely raised him, the grand marshal retained all the qualities of the private citizen. The splendor of his position had not power to dazzle or corrupt him. Duroc remained simple, natural, and independent; a warm and generous friend, a just and honorable man. I pronounce on him this eulogy without fear of contradiction."

It is not strange that Hortense, a beautiful girl of eighteen, should have fallen deeply in love with such a young soldier, twenty-nine years of age. It would seem that Duroc was equally inspired with love and admiration for Hortense. Though perhaps not positively engaged, there was such an understanding between the young lovers that a brisk correspondence was kept up during one of Duroc's embassies to the north.

Bourrienne, at that time the private secretary of Napoleon, says that this correspondence was carried on by consent through his hands. With the rapidly rising greatness of the family, there was little retirement to be enjoyed at the Tuileries or at Malmaison. The saloons of the First Consul were every evening crowded with guests. Youthful love is the same passion, and the young heart throbs with the same impulses, whether in the palace or in the cottage. When Bourrienne whispered to Hortense that he had a letter for her from Duroc, and slipped it unperceived into her hand, she would immediately retire to her room for its perusal; and the moistened eyes with which she returned to the saloon testified to the emotions with which the epistle from her lover had been read.

But Josephine had the strongest reasons which can well be imagined for opposing the connection with Duroc. She was a very loving mother. She wished to do everything in her power to promote the happiness of Hortense, but she probably was not aware how deeply the affections of her daughter were fixed upon Duroc. Her knowledge of the world also taught her that almost every young lady and every young gentleman have several loves before reaching the one which is consummated by marriage. She had another match in view for Hortense which she deemed far more eligible for her, and far more promotive of the happiness of the family.

Napoleon had already attained grandeur unsurpassed by any of the ancient kings of France. Visions of still greater power were opening before him. It was not only to him a bitter disappointment but apparently it might prove a great national calamity that he had no heir to whom he could transmit the scepter which France had placed in his hands. Upon his downfall, civil war might ravage the kingdom, as rival chieftains grasped at the crown. It was earnestly urged upon him that the interests of France imperiously demanded that, since he had no prospect of an heir by Josephine, he should obtain a divorce and marry another. It was urged that the welfare of thirty millions of people should not be sacrificed to the inclinations of two individuals.

Josephine had heard these rumors, and her life was embittered by their terrible import. A pall of gloom shrouded her sky, and anguish

The love letter.

began to gnaw at her heart amidst all the splendors of the Tuileries and the lovely retirement of Malmaison.

Napoleon's younger brother, Louis, was of nearly the same age with Hortense. He was a young man of fine personal appearance, very intelligent, of scholarly tastes, and of irreproachable character. Though pensive in temperament, he had proved himself a hero on the field of battle, and he possessed, in all respects, a very noble character. Many of the letters which he had written from Egypt to his friends in Paris had been intercepted by the British cruisers, and were published. They all bore the impress of the lofty spirit of integrity and humanity with which he was inspired. Napoleon was very fond of his brother Louis. He would surely place him in the highest positions of wealth and power. As Louis Bonaparte was remarkably domestic in his tastes and affectionate in his disposition, Josephine could not doubt that he would make Hortense happy. Apparently it was a match full of promise, brilliant, and in all respects desirable. Its crowning excellence, however, in the eye of Josephine was, that should Hortense marry Louis Bonaparte and give birth to a son, Napoleon would recognize that child as his heir. Bearing the name of Bonaparte, with the blood of the Bonapartes in his veins, and being the child of Hortense, whom he so tenderly loved as a daughter, the desires of Napoleon and of France might be satisfied. Thus the terrible divorce might be averted.

It is not probable that at this time Napoleon seriously thought of a divorce, though the air was filled with rumors put in circulation by those who were endeavoring to crowd him to it. He loved Josephine tenderly, and of course could not sympathize with her in those fears of which it was impossible for her to speak to him. Bourrienne testifies that Josephine one day said to him in confidence, veiling and at the same time revealing her fears, "This projected marriage with Duroc leaves me without support. Duroc, independent of Bonaparte's friendship, is nothing. He has neither fortune, rank, nor even reputation. He can afford me no protection against the enmity of the brothers. I must have some more certain reliance for the future. My husband loves Louis very much. If I can succeed in uniting my daughter to him, he will prove a strong counterpoise to the calumnies and persecutions of my brothers-in-law."

These remarks were repeated to Napoleon. According to Bourrienne, he replied,

"Josephine labors in vain. Duroc and Hortense love each other, and they shall be married. I am attached to Duroc. He is well born. I have given Caroline to Murat, and Pauline to Le Clerc. I can as well give Hortense to Duroc. He is as good as the others. He is general of division. Besides, I have other views for Louis."

Josephine, however, soon won the assent of Napoleon to her views, and he regarded with great satisfaction the union of Hortense with Louis. The contemplated connection with Duroc was broken off. Two young hearts were thus crushed, with cruelty quite unintentional. Duroc was soon after married to an heiress, who brought him a large fortune, and, it is said, a haughty spirit and an irritable temper, which embittered all his days.

Hortense, disappointed, heartbroken, despairing, was weary of the world. She probably never saw another happy day. Such is life.

> "Sorrows are for the sons of men,
> And weeping for earth's daughters."

Chapter IV
The Marriage of Hortense

It will be remembered that Hortense had a cousin, Stephanie, the daughter of her father's elder brother, Marquis de Beauharnais. Though Viscount de Beauharnais had espoused the popular cause in the desperate struggle of the French Revolution, the marquis was an undisguised "aristocrat." Allying himself with the king and the court, he had fled from France with the emigrant nobles. He had joined the allied army as it was marching upon his native land in the endeavor to crush out popular liberty and to reinstate the Bourbons on their throne of despotism. For this crime he was by the laws of France a traitor, doomed to the scaffold should he be captured.

The marquis, in his flight from France, had left Stephanie with her aunt Josephine. She had sent her to the school of Madame Campan in company with Hortense and Caroline Bonaparte. Louis Bonaparte was consequently often in the company of Stephanie, and fell desperately in love with her. The reader will recollect the letter which Josephine wrote to Madame Campan relative to Stephanie, which indicated that she had some serious defects of character. Still she was a brilliant girl, with great powers of pleasing when she condescended to use those powers.

Louis Bonaparte was a very pensive, meditative young man, of poetic temperament, and of unsullied purity of character. With such persons love ever becomes an all-absorbing passion. It has been well said that love is represented as a little Cupid shooting tiny arrows, whereas it should be presented as a giant shaking the world. The secrets of the heart are seldom revealed to others. Neither Napoleon nor Josephine were probably at all aware how intense and engrossing was the affection of Louis for Stephanie.

Regenerated France was then struggling, with all its concentrated energies, against the combined aristocracies of Europe. Napoleon was the leader of the popular party. The father of Stephanie was in the counsels and the army of the Allies. Already advances had been made to Napoleon, and immense bribes offered to induce him, in treachery to the people, to restore to the exiled Bourbons the scepter which the confiding people had placed in his hands. Napoleon, like all men in power, had bitter enemies, who were ever watching for an opportunity to assail him. Should his brother Louis marry a daughter of one of the old nobility, an avowed aristocrat, an emigrant, a pronounced "traitor," doomed to death, should he be captured, for waging war against his native land, it would expose Napoleon to suspicion. His enemies would have new vantage-ground from which to attack him, and in the most tender point.

Under these circumstances Napoleon contemplated with well-founded anxiety the idea of his brother's union with Stephanie. He was therefore the more ready to listen to Josephine's suggestion of the marriage of Louis and Hortense. This union in every respect seemed exceedingly desirable. Napoleon could gratify their highest ambition in assigning to them posts of opulence and honor. They could also be of great service to Napoleon in his majestic plan of redeeming all Europe from the yoke of the old feudal despotisms, and in conferring upon the peoples the new political gospel of equal rights for all men.

Napoleon had perceived this growing attachment just before he set out on the expedition to Egypt. To check it, if possible, he sent Louis on a very important mission to Toulon, where he kept him intensely occupied until he was summoned to embark for Egypt. But such love as animated the heart of Louis is deepened, not diminished, by absence. A naval officer, who was a friend of Louis, and who was aware of his attachment for Stephanie, remonstrated with him against a connection so injudicious.

"Do you know," said he, "that a marriage of this description might be highly injurious to your brother, and render him an object of suspicion to the Government, and that, too, at a moment when he is setting out on a hazardous expedition?"

But Louis was in no mood to listen to such suggestions. It would appear that Stephanie was a young lady who could very easily transfer her affections. During the absence of Louis a match was arranged between Stephanie and the Duke of Baden. The heart of Louis was hopelessly crushed. He never recovered from the blow. These were the two saddened hearts, to whom the world was shrouded in gloom, which met amidst the splendors of the Tuileries.

The genius of Napoleon and the tact of Josephine were combined to unite in marriage the disappointed and despairing lovers, Louis and Hortense. After a brief struggle, they both sadly submitted to their fate. The melancholy marriage scene is minutely described by Constant, one of the officers in the household of Napoleon. The occasion was invested with all possible splendor. A brilliant assembly attended. But as Louis led his beautiful bride to the altar, the deepest dejection marked his countenance. Hortense buried her eyes in her handkerchief and wept bitterly.

From that hour the alienation commenced. The grief-stricken bride, young, inexperienced, impulsive, made no attempt to conceal the repugnance with which she regarded the husband who had been forced upon her. On the other hand, Louis had too much pride to pursue with his attentions a bride whom he had reluctantly received, and who openly manifested her aversion to him. Josephine was very sad. Her maternal instincts revealed to her the true state of the case. Conscious that the union, which had so inauspiciously commenced, had been brought about by her, she exerted all her powers to promote friendly relations between the parties. But her counsels and her prayers were alike in vain. Louis Bonaparte, in his melancholy autobiography, writes:

"Never was there a more gloomy wedding. Never had husband and wife a stronger presentiment of a forced and ill-suited marriage. Before the ceremony, during the benediction, and ever afterwards, we both and equally felt that we were not suited to each other."

"I have seen," writes Constant, "a hundred times Madame Louis Bonaparte seek the solitude of her apartment and the bosom of a friend, there to shed her tears. She would often escape from her husband in the midst of the saloon of the First Consul, where one saw with chagrin this young woman, formerly glittering in beauty, and who gracefully performed the honors of the palace, retire into a corner or into the embrasure of a window, with some one of her intimate friends, sadly to confide her griefs. During this interview, from which she would return with her eyes red and flooded, her husband would remain pensive and silent at the end of the saloon."

Napoleon at St. Helena, referring to this painful subject, said: "Louis had been spoiled by reading the works of Rousseau. He contrived to agree with his wife only for a few months. There were faults on both sides. On the one hand, Louis was too teasing in his temper, and, on the other, Hortense was too volatile. Hortense, the devoted, the generous Hortense, was not entirely faultless in her conduct towards her husband. This I must acknowledge, in spite of all the affection I bore her, and the sincere attachment which I am sure she entertained for me. Though Louis's whimsical humors were in all probability sufficiently teasing, yet he loved Hortense. In such a case a woman should learn to subdue her own temper, and endeavor to return her husband's attachment. Had she acted in the way most conducive to her interest, she might have avoided her late lawsuit, secured happiness to herself and followed her husband to Holland. Louis would not then have fled from Amsterdam, and I should not have been compelled to unite his kingdom to mine—a measure which contributed to ruin my credit in Europe. Many other events might also have taken a different turn. Perhaps an excuse might be found for the caprice of Louis's disposition in the deplorable state of his health."

The following admirable letter from Josephine to Hortense throws additional light upon this unhappy union:

"I was deeply grieved at what I heard a few days ago. What I saw yesterday confirms and increases my distress. Why show this repugnance to Louis? Instead of rendering it the more annoying, by caprice and inequality of temper, why not endeavor to surmount it? You say he is not amiable. Everything is relative. If he is not so to you, he may be to others, and all women do not see him through the veil of dislike. As for myself, who am here altogether disinterested, I imagine that I behold him as he is—more loving, doubtless, than lovable. But this is a great and rare quality. He is generous, beneficent, affectionate. He is a good father, and if you so will, he would prove a good husband. His melancholy, and his taste for study and retirement, render him disagreeable to you. But let me ask you, is this his fault? Do you expect him to change his nature according to circumstances? Who could have foreseen his altered fortune? But, according to you, he has not even the courage to bear that fortune. This, I think, is a mistake. With his secluded habits, and his invincible love of retirement and study, he is out of place in the elevated rank to which he has been raised.

"You wish that he resembled his brother. But he must first have his brother's temperament. You have not failed to remark that almost our entire existence depends upon our health, and health upon digestion. If poor Louis's digestion were better, you would find him much more amiable. But as he is, there is nothing to justify the indifference and dislike you evince towards him. You, Hortense, who used to be so good, should continue so now, when it is most requisite. Take pity on a man who is to be pitied for what would constitute the happiness of another. Before you condemn him, think of others who, like him, have groaned beneath the burden of their greatness, and bathed with tears their diadem, which they believed had never been destined for their brow. When I advise you to love, or at least not to repulse Louis, I speak to you as an experienced wife, a fond mother, and a friend; and in these three characters, which are all equally dear to me, I tenderly embrace you."

Madame Montesson gave the first ball that took place in honor of the marriage of Louis Bonaparte and Hortense. Invitations were issued for seven hundred persons. Though there was no imperial court at that time, for Napoleon was but First Consul, yet everything was arranged on a scale of regal splendor. The foreign ambassadors were all present; and the achievements of Napoleon had been so marvelous, and his increasing grandeur was so sure, that all present vied alike in evincing homage to the whole Bonaparte family. A lady who was a guest on the occasion writes:

"Every countenance beamed with joy save that of the bride, whose profound melancholy formed a sad contrast to the happiness which she might have been expected to evince. She was covered with diamonds and flowers, and yet her countenance and manner showed nothing but regret. It was easy to foresee the mutual misery that would arise out of this ill-assorted union. Louis Bonaparte showed but little attention to his bride. Hortense, on her part, seemed to shun his very looks, lest he should read in hers the indifference she felt towards him. This indifference daily augmented in spite of the affectionate advice of Josephine, who earnestly desired to see Hortense in the possession of that happiness and peace of mind to which she was herself a stranger. But all her endeavors were unavailing."

The first child the fruit of this marriage was born in 1803, and received the name of Napoleon Charles. Both Napoleon and Josephine were rendered very happy by his birth. He was an exceedingly beautiful and promising child, and they hoped that parental endearments, lavished upon the same object, would unite father and mother more closely. Napoleon loved the child tenderly, was ever fond of caressing him, and distinctly announced his intention of making him his heir. All thoughts of the divorce were banished, and a few gleams of tremulous joy visited the heart of Josephine. But alas! these joys proved of but short duration. It was soon manifest to her anxious view that there was no hope of any cordial reconciliation between Louis and Hortense. And nothing could soothe the sorrow of Josephine's heart when she saw her daughter's happiness apparently blighted forever.

Napoleon, conscious that he had been an instrument in the bitter disappointments of Hortense and Louis, did everything in his power to requite them for the wrong. Upon attaining the imperial dignity, he appointed his brother Louis constable of France, and soon after, in 1805, governor-general of Piedmont. In 1806, Schimmelpennink, grand pensionary of Batavia, resigning his office as chief magistrate of the United Netherlands, Napoleon raised Louis to the dignity of King of Holland.

On the 18th of June, 1806, Louis and Hortense arrived in their new dominions. The exalted station to which Hortense was thus elevated did not compensate her for the sadness of separation from her beloved mother, with whom she had been so intimately associated during her whole life. The royal pair took up their residence at the Maison de Bois, a rural palace about three miles from The Hague. Here they received the various deputations, and thence made their public entrée into the capital in the midst of a scene of universal rejoicing. The pensive air of the queen did but add to the interest which she invariably excited. For a time she endeavored to drown her griefs in yielding herself to the festivities of the hour. Her fine figure, noble mien, and graceful manners fascinated all eyes and won all hearts. Her complexion was of dazzling purity, her eyes of a soft blue, and a profusion of fair hair hung gracefully upon her shoulders. Her conversation was extremely lively and vivacious, having on every occasion just the right word to say. Her dancing was said to be the perfection of grace. With such accomplishments for her station, naturally fond of society and gaiety, and with a disposition to recompense herself, for her heart's disappointment, in the love of her new subjects, she secured in a very high degree the admiration of the Hollanders.

It was at this time that Hortense composed that beautiful collection of airs called *romances* which has given her position among the ablest of musical composers. "The saloons of Paris," says a French writer, "the solitude of exile, the most remote countries, have all acknowledged the charm of these most delightful melodies, which need no royal name to enhance their reputation. It is gratifying to our pride of country to hear the airs of France sung by the Greek and by the Russian, and united to national poetry on the banks of the Thames and the Tagus. The homage thus rendered is the more flattering because the rank of the composer is unknown. It is their intrinsic merit which gives to these natural effusions of female sensibility the power of universal success. If Hortense ever experienced matrimonial felicity, it must have been at this time."

When Madame de Staël was living in exile in the old Castle of Chaumont-sur-Loire, where she was joined by her beautiful friend Madame Récamier, one of their favorite songs was that exquisite air composed by Queen Hortense upon her husband's motto, "Do what is right, come what may."

The little son of Hortense was twining himself closely around his mother's heart. He had become her idol. Napoleon was then in the zenith of his power, and it was understood that Napoleon Charles was to inherit the imperial scepter. The warmth of his heart and his daily intellectual development indicated that he would prove worthy of the station which he was destined to fill.

Shortly after the queen's arrival at The Hague, she received a New Year's present from Josephine for the young Napoleon Charles. It consisted of a large chest filled with the choicest playthings which Paris could present. The little boy was seated near a window which opened upon the park. As his mother took one after another of the playthings from the chest to exhibit to him, she was surprised and disappointed to find that he regarded them with so much indifference. His attention seemed to be very much occupied in looking out into the park. Hortense said to him, "My son, are you not grateful to your grandmamma for sending you so many beautiful presents?"

"Indeed I am, mamma," he replied. "But it does not surprise me, for grandmamma is always so good that I am used to it."

"Then you are not amused with all these pretty playthings, my son?"

Hortense

"Oh yes, mamma, but—but then I want something else."

"What is it, my darling? You know how much I love you. You may be sure that I will give it to you."

"No, mamma, I am afraid you won't. I want you to let me run about barefooted in that puddle in the avenue."

His mother of course could not grant this request, and the little fellow mourned very justly over the misfortune of being a prince, which prevented him from enjoying himself like other boys in playing in the mud.

Hortense, absorbed in her new cares, wrote almost daily to her mother, giving interesting recitals of the child. She did not, however, write as frequently to her father. Josephine wrote to her from Aix-la-Chapelle, under date of September 8th, 1804:

> "The news which you give me of Napoleon affords me great pleasure, my dear Hortense; for in addition to the very tender interest I feel for him, I appreciate all the anxieties from which you are relieved; and you know, my dear child, that your happiness will ever constitute a part of mine. The Emperor has read your letter. He has at times appeared to me wounded, in not hearing from you. He would not accuse your heart if he knew you as well as I do. But appearances are against you. Since he may suppose that you neglect him, do not lose a moment to repair the wrongs which are not intentional. Say to him that it is through discretion that you have not written to him; that your heart suffers from that law which even respect dictates; that having always manifested towards you the goodness and tenderness of a father, it will ever be your happiness to offer to him the homage of gratitude.
>
> "Speak to him also of the hope you cherish of seeing me at the period of your confinement. I cannot endure the thought of being absent from you at that time. Be sure, my Hortense, that nothing can prevent me from going to take care of you for your sake, and still more for my own. Do you speak of this also to Bonaparte, who loves you as if you were his own child. And this greatly increases my attachment for him. Adieu, my good Hortense. I embrace you with the warmest affections of my heart."

The Marriage of Hortense

Soon after this Hortense gave birth to her second child, Napoleon Louis. The health of the mother not long after the birth of the child rendered it necessary for her to visit the waters of St. Armand. It seems that little Napoleon Louis was placed under the care of a nurse where Josephine could often see him. The Empress wrote to Hortense from St. Cloud on the 20th of July, 1805:

> "My health requires that I should repose a little from the fatigues of the long journey which I have just made, and particularly from the grief which I have experienced in separating myself from Eugene in Italy. I received yesterday a letter from him. He is very well, and works hard. He greatly regrets being separated from his mother and his beloved sister. Alas! there are unquestionably many people who envy his lot, and who think him very happy. Such persons do not read his heart. In writing to you, my dear Hortense, I would only speak to you of my tenderness for you, and inform you how happy I have been to have your son Napoleon Louis with me since my return.
>
> "The Emperor, without speaking to me about it, sent to him immediately on our arrival at Fontainebleau. I was much touched by this attention on his part. He had perceived that I had need of seeing a second *yourself;* a little charming being created by thee. The child is very well. He is very happy. He eats only the soup which his nurse gives him. He never comes in when we are at the table. The Emperor caresses him very much. Eugene has given me, for you, a necklace of malachite, engraved in relief. M. Bergheim will hand you one which I purchased at Milan. It is composed of engraved amethysts, which will be very becoming upon your beautiful white skin. Give my most affectionate remembrance to your husband. Embrace for me Napoleon Charles, and rely, my dear daughter, upon the tenderness of your mother,
> "Josephine."

At midnight, on the 24th of September, 1806, Napoleon left Paris to repel a new coalition of his foes in the campaigns of Jena, Auerstadt, Eylau, and Friedland. Josephine accompanied her husband as far as Mayence, where she remained, that she might more easily receive

The little Prince Charles Napoleon.

tidings from him. Just before leaving Paris, Napoleon reviewed the Imperial Guard in the courtyard of the Tuileries. After the review he entered the saloon of Josephine. Throwing down his hat and sword upon the sofa, he took the arm of the Empress, and they together walked up and down the room, earnestly engaged in conversation. Little Napoleon Charles, who was on a visit to his grandmother, picked up the Emperor's cocked hat, placed it upon his head, and putting the sword-belt over his neck, with the dangling sword, began strutting behind the Emperor with a very military tread, attempting to whistle a martial air. Napoleon, turning around, saw the child, and catching him up in his arms, hugged and kissed him, saying to Josephine, "What a charming picture!" Josephine immediately ordered a portrait to be taken by the celebrated painter Gerard of the young prince in that costume. She intended to send it a present to the Emperor as a surprise.

The Empress remained for some time at Mayence and its environs, daily writing to the Emperor, and almost daily, sometimes twice a day, receiving letters from him. These notes were very brief, but always bore the impress of ardent affection.

On the 13th of January, 1806, Eugene was very happily married to the Princess Augusta Amélie, daughter of the Elector of Bavaria. When Josephine heard of the contemplated connection, she wrote to Hortense:

> "You know very well that the Emperor would not marry Eugene without my knowledge. Still I accept the public rumor. I should love very much to have her for a daughter-in-law. She is a charming character, and beautiful as an angel. She unites to an elegant figure the most graceful carriage I have ever known."

A few days after, on the 9th of January, she wrote from Munich:

> "I am not willing to lose a moment, my dear Hortense, in informing you that the marriage of Eugene with the daughter of the Elector of Bavaria is just definitely arranged. You will appreciate, as I do, all the value of this new proof of the attachment which the Emperor manifests for your brother. Nothing in the world could be more agreeable to me

than this alliance. The young princess unites to a charming figure all the qualities which can render a woman interesting and lovely. The marriage is not to be celebrated here, but in Paris. Thus you will be able to witness the happiness of your brother, and mine will be perfect, since I shall find myself united to both of my dear children."

The arrangements were changed subsequently, and the nuptials were solemnized in Munich. Napoleon wrote as follows to Hortense:

"Munich, January 9th, 1806.
"MY DAUGHTER,—Eugene arrives tomorrow, and is to be married in four days. I should have been very happy if you could have attended his marriage, but there is no longer time. The Princess Augusta is tall, beautiful, and full of good qualities, and you will have, in all respects, a sister worthy of you. A thousand kisses to M. Napoleon.
"NAPOLEON."

The Empress, after remaining some time at Mayence, as the campaign on the banks of the Vistula was protracted, returned to Paris. In a state of great anxiety with regard to her husband, she took up her residence at St. Cloud. Under date of March, 1807, she wrote to her daughter, then queen of Holland, residing at The Hague:

"I have received much pleasure in speaking of you with M. Jansens. I perceive, from what he tells me respecting Holland, that the king is very much beloved, and that you share in the general affection. This renders me happy. My health is very good at the present moment, but my heart is always sad.
"All the private letters which I have seen agree in the declaration that the Emperor exposed himself very much at the battle of Eylau. I frequently receive tidings from him, and sometimes two letters a day. This is a great consolation, but it does not replace him."

That Napoleon, in the midst of the ten thousand cares of so arduous a campaign, could have found time to write daily to

Josephine, and often twice a day, is surely extraordinary. There are not many husbands, it is to be feared, who are so thoughtful of the anxieties of an absent wife.

Early in May the Empress received the portrait, of which we have spoken, of her idolized grandchild, Napoleon Charles, in his amusing military costume. She was intending to send it as a pleasing memorial to the Emperor in his distant encampment.

Just then she received the dreadful tidings that little Napoleon Charles had been taken sick with the croup, and, after the illness of but a few hours, had died. It was the 5th of May, 1807. Josephine was in Paris; Hortense at The Hague, in Holland; Napoleon was hundreds of leagues distant in the north, with his army almost buried in snow upon the banks of the Vistula.

The world perhaps has never witnessed the death of a child which has caused so much anguish. Hortense did not leave her son for a moment, as the terrible disease advanced to its termination. When he breathed his last she seemed completely stunned. Not a tear dimmed her eye. Not a word, not a moan was uttered. Like a marble statue, she sat upon the sofa where the child had died, gazing around her with a look of wild, amazed, delirious agony. With much difficulty she was taken from the room, being removed on the sofa upon which she reclined. Her anguish was so great that for some time it was feared that reason was dethroned, and that the blow would prove fatal. Her limbs were rigid, and her dry and glassy eye was riveted upon vacancy. At length, in the endeavor to bring her out from this dreadful state, the lifeless body of the child, dressed for the grave, was brought in and placed in the lap of its mother. The pent-up anguish of Hortense now found momentary relief in a flood of tears, and in loud and uncontrollable sobbings.

The anguish of Josephine surpassed, if possible, even that of Hortense. The Empress knew that Napoleon had selected this child as his heir; that consequently the terrible divorce was no longer to be thought of. In addition to the loss of one she so tenderly loved, rose the fear that his death would prove to her the greatest of earthly calamities. For three days she could not leave her apartment, and did nothing but weep.

The sad intelligence was conveyed to Napoleon in his cheerless encampment upon the Vistula. As he received the tidings he uttered not a word. Sitting down in silence, he buried his face in his hand,

Hortense

and for a long time seemed lost in painful musings. No one ventured to disturb his grief with attempted consolation.

As soon as Josephine was able to move, she left Paris to visit her bereaved, heartbroken daughter. But her strength failed her by the way, and when she reached Luchen, a palace near Brussels, she was able to proceed no farther. She wrote as follows to Hortense:

"Luchen, May 14th, 1807—10 o'clock P.M.

"I have arrived this moment at the chateau of Luchen, my dear daughter. It is there I write to you, and there I await you. Come to restore me to life. Your presence is necessary to me, and you must also feel the need of seeing me, that you may weep with your mother. I earnestly wish to proceed farther, but my strength has failed me, and moreover I have not had time to apprise the Emperor. I have found strength to come thus far. I hope you also will find strength to come and see your mother."

Hortense immediately repaired to Luchen to seek a mother's sympathy. With Josephine she returned to Paris, and soon after, by the entreaties of her physician, continued her journey to take the waters of a mineral spring in the south of France, seeking a change of climate and of scene. Josephine remained in the depths of sorrow at St. Cloud. On the same day in which Josephine arrived at Luchen, the Emperor wrote to her from the Vistula as follows:

"Finckenstein, May 14th, 1807.

"I can appreciate the grief which the death of poor Napoleon has caused. You can understand the anguish which I experience. I could wish that I were with you, that you might become moderate and discreet in your grief. You have had the happiness of never losing any children. But it is one of the conditions and sorrows attached to suffering humanity. Let me hear that you have become reasonable and tranquil. Would you magnify my anguish?"

Two days after Napoleon wrote the Empress:

"I have received your letter of the sixth of May. I see in it already the injury which you are suffering, and I fear that you are not reasonable, and that you afflict yourself too much from the calamity which has befallen us.

"Adieu my love. Entirely thine,

"Napoleon."

Again, after the lapse of four days, he wrote:

"I have received your letter of the tenth of May. I see that you have gone to Luchen. I think that you may rest there a fortnight. That will give much pleasure to the Belgians, and will serve to divert your mind. I see with pain that you are not wise. Grief has bounds which it should not pass. Preserve yourself for your friend, and believe in all my affection."

On the same day the Emperor wrote as follows to Hortense:

"Finckenstein, May 20th, 1807.

"My Daughter,—Everything which reaches me from The Hague informs me that you are unreasonable. However legitimate may be your grief, it should have its bounds. Do not impair your health. Seek consolation. Know that life is strewn with so many dangers, and may be the source of so many calamities, that death is by no means the greatest of evils.

"Your affectionate father,

"Napoleon."

It is to be borne in mind that these brief epistles were written from the midst of one of the most arduous of campaigns. Four days after this, on the 24th, Napoleon wrote to Josephine:

"I have received your letter from Luchen. I see with pain that your grief is still unabated, and that Hortense has not yet arrived. She is unreasonable, and does not merit that one should love her, since she loves only her children. Strive to calm yourself, and give me no more pain. For every irremediable evil we should find consolation. Adieu, my love.

"Wholly thine,

"Napoleon."

After two days again the Emperor wrote to Josephine:

> "I have received your letter of the 16th, and see with pleasure that Hortense has arrived at Luchen. I am indeed grieved by what you tell me of the state of stupor in which she still continues. She should have more fortitude, and should govern herself. I cannot conceive why they should wish her to go to the springs. Her attention would be much more diverted at Paris, and she would find there more consolation. Control yourself. Be cheerful, and take care of your health. Adieu, my love. I share deeply in all your griefs. It is painful to me that I am not with you.
>
> "Napoleon."

It will be remembered that Hortense had another child, then but an infant, by the name of Napoleon Louis. This child subsequently married a daughter of Joseph Bonaparte, and died in a campaign in Italy, as he espoused the popular cause in the endeavor to throw off the yoke of Austria. The third and only surviving child, Louis Napoleon, now Emperor of the French, was not then born.

We have previously alluded in this history to a niece of Madame Campan by the name of Adèle Auguié, who was the intimate friend and companion of Hortense in her schooldays. Schoolgirl attachments, though often very ardent, are not generally very lasting. This one, however, proved of lifelong duration. Adèle became Madame de Broc. There is an allusion to her in the following letter. We shall hereafter have occasion to refer to her in describing the disaster which terminated her life. It was the latter part of May when Hortense left her mother to journey to the south of France. Soon after her departure Josephine wrote to her as follows:

> "St. Cloud, May 27th, 1807.
>
> "I have wept much since your departure, my dear Hortense. This separation has been very painful to me. Nothing can give me courage to support it but the certainty that the journey will do you good. I have received tidings from you, through Madame Broc. I pray you to thank her for that attention, and to request her to write to me when you may be unable to write yourself. I had also news from your

son. He is at the chateau of Luchen, very well, and awaiting the arrival of the king. He shares very keenly in our griefs. I have need of this consolation, for I have had none other since your departure. Always alone by myself, every moment dwelling upon the subject of our affliction, my tears flow incessantly. Adieu, my beloved child. Preserve yourself for a mother who loves you tenderly."

Soon after this Josephine went for a short time to Malmaison. On the 2d of June Napoleon wrote to her from that place the following letter, enclosing also one for Hortense.

"My Love,—I have learned of your arrival at Malmaison. I am displeased with Hortense. She does not write me a word. Everything which you say to me of her gives me pain. Why is it that you have not been able a little to console her? You weep. I hope that you will control your feelings, that I may not find you overwhelmed with sadness. I have been at Dantzic for two days. The weather is very fine, and I am well. I think more of you than you can think of one who is absent. Adieu my love. My most affectionate remembrance. Send the enclosed letter to Hortense."

The letter to Hortense to which Napoleon refers, was as follows:

"Dantzic, June 2d, 1807.

"My Daughter,—You have not written me a word in your well-founded and great affliction. You have forgotten everything as if you had no other loss to endure. I am informed that you no longer love; that you are indifferent to everything. I perceive it by your silence. This is not right, Hortense. It is not what you promised me. Your child was everything to you. Had I been at Malmaison, I should have shared your anguish. But I should also have wished that you would restore yourself to your best friends. Adieu, my daughter. Be cheerful. We must learn resignation. Cherish your health, that you may be able to fulfill all your duties. My wife is very sad in view of your condition. Do not add to her anguish."

Hortense

The next day, June 3d, the Emperor wrote to Josephine:

"All the letters which come to me from St. Cloud say that you weep continually. This is not right. It is necessary to control one's self and to be contented. Hortense is entirely wrong. What you write me about her is pitiful. Adieu, my love. Believe in the affection with which I cherish you."

The next day Josephine wrote from the palace of St. Cloud to Hortense, who was then at the waters of Cauterets:

"Your letter has greatly consoled me, my dear Hortense, and the tidings of your health, which I have received from your ladies, contribute very much to render me more tranquil. The Emperor has been deeply affected. In all his letters he seeks to give me fortitude, but I know that this severe affliction has been keenly felt by him.

"The king[1] arrived yesterday at St. Leu. He has sent me word that he will come to see me today. He will leave the little one with me during his absence. You know how dearly I love that child, and the solicitude I feel for him. I hope that the king will follow the same route which you have taken. It will be, my dear Hortense, a consolation to you both to see each other again. All the letters which I have received from him since his departure are full of his attachment for you. Your heart is too affectionate not to be touched by this. Adieu, my dear child. Take care of your health. Mine can never be established till I shall no longer suffer for those whom I love. I embrace you tenderly.

"JOSEPHINE."

Two days after this, on the 6th, the Emperor wrote the Empress:

"I am very well, my love. Your letter of yesterday gave me much pain. It appears that you are continually sad, and that you are not reasonable. The weather is very bad. Adieu, my

---

[1] The husband of Hortense, King of Holland. He was then very sick, suffering from an attack of paralysis. St. Leu was a beautiful estate he owned in France. He had with him his second and then only living child, Napoleon Louis. Leaving him with his grandmother, he repaired to Cauterets, where he joined Hortense, his wife.

love. I love you and desire to hear that you are cheerful and contented."

On the 11th of June, Josephine again wrote to Hortense:

"Your son is remarkably well. He amuses me much; he is so pleasant. I find he has all the endearing manners of the poor child over whose loss we weep."

Again she wrote, probably the next day, in answer to a letter from Hortense:

"Your letter has affected me deeply, my dear daughter. I see how profound and unvarying is your grief. And I perceive it still more sensibly by the anguish which I experience myself. We have lost that which in every respect was the most worthy to be loved. My tears flow as on the first day. Our grief is too well-founded for reason to be able to cause it to cease. Nevertheless, my dear Hortense, you should moderate it. You are not alone in the world. There still remains to you a husband and a mother, whose tender love you well know, and you have too much sensibility to regard all that with coldness and indifference. Think of us; and let that memory calm another well-grounded and grievous. I rely upon your attachment for me and upon the strength of your mind. I hope also that the journey and the waters will do you good. Your son is remarkably well. He is a charming child. My health is a little better, but you know that it depends upon yours. Adieu. I embrace you.
"JOSEPHINE."

On the 16th of June, Napoleon again wrote to Hortense from his distant encampment:

"MY DAUGHTER,—I have received your letter dated Orleans. Your griefs touch my heart, but I could wish that you would summon more fortitude. To live is to suffer, and the sincere man suffers incessantly to retain the mastery over himself. I do not love to see you unjust towards the little Napoleon Louis, and towards all your friends. Your mother

Hortense

and I had cherished the hope of being more than we are in your heart. I have gained a great victory on the 14th of June.[1] I am well and love you very much. Adieu, my daughter. I embrace you with my whole heart."

The above extracts from the private correspondence of Napoleon and Josephine reveal, more clearly than anything else could possibly do, the anguish with which Hortense was oppressed. They also exhibit, in a very interesting light, the affectionate relationship which existed between the members of the Imperial family. The authenticity of the letters is beyond all possible question. How much more charitable should we be could we but fully understand the struggles and the anguish to which all human hearts are exposed.

---

[1] Victory of Friedland.

Chapter V
Birth of Louis Napoleon and the Divorce of Josephine

The latter part of July, 1807, Hortense, in the state of anguish which the preceding chapter develops, was, with her husband, at the waters of Cauterets, in the south of France. They were united by the ties of a mutual grief. Napoleon was more than a thousand miles away in the north of Europe. In considerably less than a year from that date, on the 20th of April, 1808, Hortense gave birth, in Paris to her third child, Louis Napoleon, now Napoleon III, Emperor of the French. Josephine was then at Bordeaux, and wrote as follows to Hortense:

"Bordeaux, April 23d, 1808.

"I am, my dear Hortense, in an excess of joy. The tidings of your happy accouchement were brought to me yesterday by M. de Villeneuve. I felt my heart beat the moment I saw him enter. But I cherished the hope that he had only good tidings to bring me, and my presentiments did not deceive me. I have received a second letter, which assures me that you are very well, and also your son. I know that Napoleon will console himself in not having a sister, and that he already loves very much his brother. Embrace them both for me. But I must not write you too long a letter from fear of fatiguing you. Take care of yourself with the utmost caution. Do not receive too much company at present. Let me hear from you every day. I await tidings from you with as much impatience as I love you with tenderness.

"Josephine."

The birth of this prince, Louis Napoleon, whose renown as Napoleon III now fills the world, and respecting whose character and achievements there is so wonderful a diversity of sentiment among intelligent men, took place in Paris. Napoleon was at that time upon the highest pinnacle of prosperity. The Allies, vanquished in every conflict, seemed disposed to give up the attempt to reinstate the Bourbons upon the throne of France. The birth of Louis Napoleon, as a prince of the Empire, in the direct line of hereditary descent, was welcomed by the guns of the Invalides, and by military salutes all along the lines of the Imperial army, from Hamburg to Rome, and from the Pyrenees to the Danube. The important event was thus announced in the *Moniteur* of April 21st:

"Yesterday, at one o'clock, her Majesty the Queen of Holland was safely delivered of a prince. In conformity with Article 40, of the Act of the Constitution of 28 Floreal, year 12, the Chancellor of the Empire attested the birth, and wrote immediately to the Emperor, the Empress, and the King of Holland, to communicate the intelligence. At five o'clock in the evening, the act of birth was received by the arch chancellor, assisted by his eminence, Reynault de St. Jean d'Angely, minister of state and state secretary of the Imperial family. In the absence of the Emperor, the newborn prince has not yet received his name. This will be provided for by an ulterior act, according to the orders of his Majesty."

By a decree of the Senate, these two children of Louis Bonaparte and Hortense were declared heirs to the Imperial throne, should Napoleon and his elder brother Joseph die without children. This decree of the Senate was submitted to the acceptation of the French people. With wonderful unanimity it was adopted. There were 3,521,675 votes in the affirmative, and but 2599 in the negative.

Napoleon ever manifested the deepest interest in these two children. At the time of the birth of Louis Napoleon he was at Bayonne, arranging with the Spanish princes for the transfer of the crown of Spain to Joseph Bonaparte. Josephine was at Bordeaux. From this interview he passed, in his meteoric flight, to the Congress of Kings at Erfurt, but a few miles from the battlefield of Jena. It was here that the celebrated historian Müller met the Emperor and gave the following testimony as to the impression which his presence produced upon his mind:

"Quite impartially and truly, as before God, I must say, that the variety of his knowledge, the acuteness of his observation, the solidity of his understanding, filled me with astonishment. His manner of speaking to me inspired me with love for him. It was one of the most remarkable days of my life. By his genius and his disinterested goodness he has conquered me also."

Hortense, with a saddened spirit, now lived in great seclusion, devoting herself almost exclusively to the education of her two sons, Napoleon Louis and Louis Napoleon. Her bodily health was feeble, and she was most of the time deeply dejected. In May, 1809, Hortense, without consulting the Emperor, who was absent in Germany, took the two princes with her to the baths of Baden, where they were exposed to the danger of being seized and held as hostages by the Austrians. The solicitude of the Emperor for them may be seen in the following letter:

"Ebersdorf, May 28th, 1809.

"My Daughter,—I am very much displeased (*très mécontent*), that you should have left France without my permission, and particularly that you should have taken my nephews from France. Since you are at the waters of Baden, remain there. But in one hour after the reception of this letter, send my two nephews to Strasbourg, near to the Empress. They ought never to leave France. It is the first time that I have had occasion to be dissatisfied with you. But you ought not to dispose of my nephews without my permission. You ought to perceive the mischievous effects which that may produce.

"Since the waters of Baden are beneficial to you, you can remain there some days. But I repeat to you, do not delay for a moment sending my nephews to Strasbourg. Should the Empress go to the waters of Plombières they can accompany her there. But they ought never to cross the bridge of Strasbourg. Your affectionate father,

"Napoleon."

This letter was sent to Josephine to be transmitted by her to Hortense. She received it on the first of June, and immediately sent it to her daughter, with a letter which implies that Hortense had already anticipated the wishes of Napoleon, and had sent the princes, after a brief visit, to Josephine at Strasbourg. Soon after this it would seem that little Louis Napoleon, who was evidently the favorite of his grandmother, perhaps because he was more with her, accompanied Josephine to St Cloud. About a fortnight after this she wrote to Hortense from that palace:

"I am happy to have your son with me. He is charming. I am attached to him more and more, in thinking he will be a solace to you. His little reasons amuse me much. He grows every day, and his complexion is very fine. I am far from you, but I frequently embrace your son, and love to imagine to myself that it is my dear daughter whom I embrace."

And now we approach that almost saddest of earth's tragedies, the divorce of Josephine—the great wrong and calamity of Napoleon's life. The event had so important a bearing upon the character and the destiny of Hortense as to demand a brief recital here.

It is often difficult to judge of the *motives* of human actions; but at times circumstances are such that it is almost impossible to misjudge the causes which lead to conduct. General Savary, Duke of Rovigo, the intimate personal friend of the Emperor, and one better acquainted with his secret thoughts than any other person, gives the following account of this momentous and fatal act:

"A thousand idle stories have been related concerning the Emperor's motives for breaking the bonds he had contracted upwards of fifteen years before, and separating from one who was the partner of his life during the most stormy events of his glorious career. It was ascribed to his ambition to connect himself with royal blood; and malevolence has delighted in spreading the report that to this consideration he had sacrificed every other. This opinion was quite erroneous, and he was as unfairly dealt with, upon the subject, as all persons are who happen to be placed above the level of mankind.

"Nothing can be more true than that the sacrifice of the object of his affections was the most painful that he experienced throughout his life; and that he would have preferred adopting any course than the one to which he was driven by the motives which I am about to relate. Public opinion in general was unjust to the Emperor, when he placed the imperial crown upon his head. A feeling of personal ambition was supposed to be the mainspring of all his actions. This was, however, a very mistaken impression. I have already mentioned with what reluctance he had altered the form of government, and that if he had not been apprehensive that the State would fall again a prey to those dissensions which are inseparable from an elective form of government, he would not have changed an order of things which appeared to have been the first solid conquest achieved by the revolution. Ever since he had brought back the nation to monarchical principles, he had neglected no means of consolidating institutions which permanently secured those principles, and yet firmly established the superiority of modern ideas over antiquated customs. Differences of opinion could no longer create any disturbance respecting the form of government, when his career should be closed.

"But this was not enough. It was further requisite that the line of inheritance should be defined in so clear a manner that, at his death, no pretense might be made for the contention of any claimants to the throne. For if such a misfortune were to take place, the least foreign intervention would have sufficed to revive a spirit of discord among us. This feeling of personal ambition consisted in this case, in a desire to hand his work down to posterity, and to resign to his successor a state resting upon his numerous trophies for its stability. He could not have been blind to the fact, that the perpetual warfare into which a jealousy of his strength had plunged him, had, in reality, no other object than his own downfall, because with him must necessarily crumble that gigantic power which was no longer upheld by revolutionary energy he himself had repressed.

"The Emperor had not any children. The Empress had two, but he never could have entertained a thought of them without exposing himself to the most serious inconveniences. I believe, however, that if the two children of Josephine had been the only ones in his family, he would have made some arrangement for securing the inheritance to Eugene. He however dismissed the idea of appointing him his heir, because he had nearer relations, and it would have given rise to dissensions which it was his principal object to avoid. He also considered the necessity in which he was placed of forming an alliance sufficiently powerful, in order that, in the event of his system being at any time threatened, that alliance might be a resting-point, and save it from total ruin. He likewise hoped that it would be the means of putting to an end that series of wars, of which he was desirous, above all things, to avoid a recurrence. These were the motives which determined him to break a union so long contracted. He wished it less for himself than for the purpose of interesting a powerful state in the maintenance of the order of things established in France. He reflected often on the mode of making this communication to the Empress. Still he was reluctant to speak to her. He was apprehensive of the consequences of her tenderness of feeling. His heart was never proof against the shedding of tears."

The arch-chancellor Cambaceres states that Napoleon communicated to him the resolution he had adopted; alluded to the reasons for the divorce, spoke of the anguish which the stern necessity caused his affections, and declared his intention to invest the act with forms the most affectionate and the most honorable to Josephine.

"I will have nothing," said he, "which can resemble a repudiation; nothing but a mere dissolution of the conjugal tie, founded upon mutual consent; a consent itself founded upon the interests of the empire. Josephine is to be provided with a palace in Paris, with a princely residence in the country with an income of six hundred thousand dollars, and is to occupy the first rank among the princesses, after the future Empress. I wish ever to keep her near me as my best and most affectionate friend."

Josephine was in some degree aware of the doom which was impending, and her heart was consumed by unmitigated grief. Hortense, who also was heart-stricken and world-weary, was entreated by the Emperor to prepare her mother for the sad tidings. She did so, but very imperfectly. At last the fatal hour arrived in which it was necessary for the Emperor to make the dreaded announcement to the Empress. They were both at Fontainebleau, and Hortense was with her mother. For some time there had been much constraint in the intercourse between the Emperor and Empress; he dreading to make the cruel communication, and her heart lacerated with anguish in the apprehension of receiving it.

It was the last day of November, 1809, cold and cheerless. Napoleon and Josephine dined alone in silence, not a word being spoken during the repast. At the close of the meal, Napoleon, pale and trembling, took the hand of the Empress and said:

"Josephine, my own good Josephine, you know how I have loved you. It is to you alone that I owe the few moments of happiness I have known in the world. Josephine, my destiny is stronger than my will. My dearest affections must yield to the welfare of France."

All-expected as the blow was, it was none the less dreadful. Josephine fell, apparently lifeless, to the floor. The Count de Beaumont was immediately summoned, and, with the aid of Napoleon, conveyed Josephine to her apartment. Hortense came at once to her mother, whom she loved so tenderly. The anguish of the scene overcame her. In respectful, though reproachful tones, she said to the Emperor, "My mother will descend from the throne, as she ascended it, in obedience to your will. Her children, content to renounce grandeurs which have not made them happy, will gladly go and devote their lives to comforting the best and the most affectionate of mothers."

Napoleon was entirely overcome. He sat down and wept bitterly. Raising his eyes swimming in tears to his daughter, he said:

"Do not leave me, Hortense. Stay by me with Eugene. Help me to console your mother and render her calm, resigned, and even happy in remaining my friend, while she ceases to be my wife."

Eugene was summoned from Italy. Upon his arrival his sister threw herself into his arms, and, after a brief interview of mutual anguish, led him to their beloved mother. After a short interview with her, he repaired to the cabinet of the Emperor. In respectful terms, but firm and very sad, he inquired if Napoleon intended to obtain a divorce from the Empress. Napoleon, who tenderly loved his noble son, could only reply with the pressure of the hand. Eugene immediately recoiled and, withdrawing his hand, said:

"In that case, Sire, permit me to retire from your service."

"How," exclaimed Napoleon, looking sadly upon him. "Will you, my adopted son, forsake me?"

"Yes, Sire," Eugene replied. "The son of her who is no longer Empress, cannot remain viceroy. I will follow my mother into her retreat. She must now find her consolation in her children."

Tears filled the eyes of the Emperor. "You know," said he, "the stern necessity which compels this measure. Will you forsake me? Who then, should I have a son, the object of my desires and preserver of my interests, who will watch over the child when I am absent? If I die, who will prove to him a father? Who will bring him up? Who is to make a man of him?"

Napoleon and Eugene then retired to the garden, and for a long time walked, arm in arm, up and down one of its avenues, engaged in earnest conversation. Josephine, with a mother's love, could not forget the interests of her children, even in her own anguish.

"The Emperor," she said to Eugene, "is your benefactor, your more than father; to whom you are indebted for everything, and to whom therefore you owe boundless obedience."

A fortnight passed away and the 15th of December arrived; the day appointed for the consummation of this cruel sacrifice.

The affecting scene transpired in the grand saloon of the palace of the Tuileries. All the members of the imperial family were present. Eugene and Hortense were with their mother, sustaining her with their sympathy and love. An extreme pallor overspread the countenance of Napoleon, as he addressed the assembled dignitaries of the empire.

"The political interests of my monarchy," said he, "and the wishes of my people, which have constantly guided my actions, require that I should transmit to an heir, inheriting my love for the people, the throne on which Providence has placed me. For many years I have lost all hope of having children by my beloved spouse the Empress Josephine. It is this consideration which induces me to sacrifice the dearest affections of my heart, to consult only the good of my subjects, and to desire the dissolution of our marriage. Arrived at the age of forty years, I may indulge the reasonable hope of living long enough to rear, in the spirit of my own thoughts and disposition, the children with which it may please Providence to bless me. God knows how much such a determination has cost my heart. But there is no sacrifice too great for my courage when it is proved to be for the interest of France. Far from having any cause of complaint, I have nothing to say but in praise of the attachment and tenderness of my beloved wife. She has embellished fifteen years of my life, and the remembrance of them will be forever engraven on my heart. She was crowned by my hand. She shall always retain the rank and title of Empress. Above all, let her never doubt my affection, or regard me but as her best and dearest friend."

Josephine now endeavored to fulfill her part in this sad drama. Unfolding a paper, she vainly strove to read her assent to the divorce. But tears blinded her eyes and emotion choked her voice. Handing the paper to a friend and sobbing aloud, she sank into a chair and buried her face in her handkerchief. Her friend, M. Reynaud, read the paper, which was as follows:

"With the permission of my august and dear spouse, I must declare that, retaining no hope of having children who may satisfy the requirements of his policy and the interests of France, I have the pleasure of giving him the greatest proof of attachment and devotedness which was ever given on earth. I owe all to his bounty. It was his hand that crowned me, and on his throne I have received only manifestations of love and affection from the French people. I respond to all the sentiments of the Emperor, in consenting to the dissolution of a marriage which is now an obstacle to the happiness of France, by depriving it of the blessing of being one day governed by the descendants of that great man who was evidently raised up by Providence to efface the evils of a terrible revolution, and to restore the altar, the throne, and social order. But the dissolution of my marriage will in no respect change the sentiments of my heart. The Emperor will ever find in me his best friend. I know how much this act, commanded by policy and exalted interests, has rent his heart. But we both glory in the sacrifices we make for the good of the country."

"After these words," says Thiers, "the noblest ever uttered under such circumstances—for never, it must be confessed, did vulgar passions less prevail in an act of this kind—Napoleon, embracing Josephine, led her to her own apartment, where he left her, almost fainting, in the arms of her children."

The next day the Senate was convened in the grand saloon to sanction the legal consummation of the divorce. Eugene presided. As he announced the desire of the Emperor and Empress for the dissolution of their marriage, he said: "The tears of his Majesty at this separation are sufficient for the glory of my mother." The description of the remaining scenes of this cruel tragedy we repeat from Abbott's *The Life of Napoleon Bonaparte.*

"The Emperor, dressed in the robes of state, and pale as a statue of marble, leaned against a pillar, careworn and wretched. Folding his arms upon his breast, with his eyes fixed upon vacancy, he stood in gloomy silence. It was a funereal scene. The low hum of mournful voices alone disturbed the stillness of the room. A circular table was placed in the center of the apartment. Upon it there was a writing apparatus of gold. A vacant armchair stood before the table. The company gazed silently upon it as the instrument of the most soul-harrowing execution.

"A side door opened, and Josephine entered. Her face was as white as the simple muslin robe which she wore. She was leaning upon the arm of Hortense, who, not possessing the fortitude of her mother, was sobbing convulsively. The whole assembly, upon the entrance of Josephine, instinctively arose. All were moved to tears. With her own peculiar grace, Josephine advanced to the seat provided for her. Leaning her pale forehead upon her hand, she

Hortense

The divorce announced.

listened with the calmness of stupor to the reading of the act of separation. The convulsive sobbings of Hortense, mingled with the subdued and mournful tones of the reader's voice, added to the tragic impressiveness of the scene. Eugene, pale and trembling, stepped forward and took a position by the side of his adored mother, to give her the moral support of his near presence.

"As soon as the reading of the act of separation was finished, Josephine, for a moment, in anguish pressed her handkerchief to her eyes, and rising, in tones clear, musical, but tremulous with repressed emotion, pronounced the oath of acceptance. She sat down, took the pen, and affixed her signature to the deed which sundered the dearest hopes and the fondest ties which human hearts can feel. Eugene could endure this anguish no longer. His brain reeled, his heart ceased to beat, and fainting, he fell senseless to the floor. Josephine and Hortense retired, with the attendants who bore out the inanimate form of the affectionate son and brother. It was a fitting termination of the heartrending yet sublime tragedy.

"Josephine remained in her chamber overwhelmed with speechless grief. A somber night darkened over the city, oppressed by the gloom of this cruel sacrifice. The hour arrived at which Napoleon usually retired for sleep. The Emperor, restless and wretched, had just placed himself in the bed from which he had ejected his faithful and devoted wife, when the private door of his chamber was slowly opened, and Josephine tremblingly entered.

"Her eyes were swollen with weeping, her hair disordered, and she appeared in all the dishabille of unutterable anguish. Hardly conscious of what she did, in the delirium of her woe, she tottered into the middle of the room and approached the bed of her former husband. Then irresolutely stopping, she buried her face in her hands and burst into a flood of tears.

"A feeling of delicacy seemed, for a moment, to have arrested her steps—a consciousness that she had *now* no right to enter the chamber of Napoleon. In another moment all the pent-up love of her heart burst forth, and forgetting everything in the fullness of her anguish, she threw herself upon the bed, clasped Napoleon's neck in her arms, and exclaiming, 'My husband! my husband!' sobbed as though her heart were breaking. The imperial spirit of Napoleon was entirely vanquished. He also wept convulsively. He assured Josephine of his love—of his ardent, undying love. In every way he tried to soothe and comfort her. For some time they remained locked in each other's embrace. The valet-de-chambre, who was still present, was dismissed, and for an hour Napoleon and Josephine continued together in this their last private interview. Josephine then, in the experience of an intensity of anguish such as few human hearts have ever known, parted forever from the *husband* whom she had so long and so faithfully loved."

Josephine having withdrawn, an attendant entered the apartment to remove the lights. He found the Emperor so buried beneath the bedclothes as to be invisible. Not a word was uttered. The lights were removed, and the unhappy monarch was left alone in darkness and silence to the melancholy companionship of his own thoughts. The next morning the death-like pallor of his cheek, his sunken eye, and the haggard expression of his countenance, attested that the Emperor had passed the night in sleeplessness and in suffering.

The grief of Napoleon was unquestionably sincere. It could not but be so. He was influenced by no vagrant passion. He had formed no new attachment. He truly loved Josephine. He consequently resolved to retire for a time to the seclusion of Trianon, at Versailles. He seemed desirous that the externals of mourning should accompany an event so mournful.

"The orders for the departure for Trianon," writes the Baron Meneval, Napoleon's private secretary, "had been previously given. When in the morning the Emperor was informed that his carriages were ready, he took his hat and said, 'Meneval, come with me.' I followed him by the little winding staircase which, from his cabinet, communicated with the apartment of the Empress. Josephine was alone, and appeared absorbed in the most melancholy reflections. At the noise which we made in entering, she eagerly rose and threw herself sobbing upon the neck of the Emperor. He pressed her to his bosom with the most ardent embraces.

"In the excess of her emotion she fainted. I rang the bell for succor. The Emperor wishing to avoid the renewal of scenes of anguish which he could no longer alleviate, placed the Empress in my arms as soon as she began to revive. Directing me not to leave her, he hastily retired to his carriage which was waiting for him at the door. The Empress, perceiving the departure of the Emperor, redoubled her tears and moans. Her women placed her upon a sofa. She seized my hands, and frantically urged me to entreat Napoleon not to forget her, and to assure him that her love would survive every event.

"She made me promise to write her immediately on my arrival at Trianon, and to see that the Emperor wrote to her also. She could hardly consent to let me go, as if my departure would break the last tie which still connected her with the Emperor. I left her, deeply moved by the exhibition of a grief so true and an attachment so sincere. I was profoundly saddened during my ride, and I could not refrain from deploring the rigorous exigencies of state which rudely sundered the ties of a long-tried affection, to impose another union offering only uncertainties. Having arrived at Trianon, I gave the Emperor a faithful account of all that had transpired after his departure. He was still oppressed by the melancholy scenes through which he had passed. He dwelt upon the noble qualities of Josephine, and upon the sincerity of the affection which she cherished for him. He ever after preserved for her the most tender attachment. The same evening he wrote to her a letter to console her solitude." The letter was as follows:

"My love, I found you today more feeble than you ought to be. You have exhibited much fortitude, and it is necessary that you should still continue to sustain yourself. You must not yield to funereal melancholy. Strive to be tranquil, and, above, all, to preserve your health, which is so precious to me. If you are attached to me, if you love me, you must maintain your energy and strive to be cheerful. You cannot doubt my constancy and my tender affection. You know too well all the sentiments with which I regard you to suppose that I can be happy if you are unhappy, that I can be serene if you are agitated. Adieu, my love. Sleep well. Believe that I wish it.
"NAPOLEON."

After the departure of the Emperor, at eleven o'clock in the morning all the household of the Tuileries were assembled upon the grand staircase, to witness the retirement of their beloved mistress from the scenes where she had so long been the brightest ornament. Josephine descended from her apartment veiled from head to foot. Her emotions were too deep for utterance. Silently she waved an adieu to the affectionate and weeping friends who surrounded her. A close carriage with six horses was before the door. She entered it,

Hortense

sank back upon the cushions, buried her face in her handkerchief, and, sobbing bitterly, left the Tuileries forever.

After the divorce, Josephine spent most of her time at the beautiful chateau of Malmaison, which had been assigned to her, or at the palace of Navarre, which was embellished for her at an expense of two hundred thousand dollars. She retained the title of Empress, and received a jointure of about six hundred thousand dollars a year. Almost daily letters were exchanged between her and the Emperor, and he frequently visited her. But from motives of delicacy he never saw her alone. We know of nothing more pathetic in history than the gleams we get of these interviews, as revealed in the *Confidential Letters of Napoleon and Josephine,* whose publication was authorized by Queen Hortense, after the death of her mother. Josephine, in the following words, describes one of these interviews at Malmaison. It was after the marriage with Maria Louisa.

"I was one day painting a violet, a flower which recalled to my memory my more happy days, when one of my women ran towards me and made a sign by placing her finger upon her lips. The next moment I was overpowered—I beheld Napoleon. He threw himself with transport into the arms of his old friend. Oh, then I was convinced that he could still love me; for that man really loved me. It seemed impossible for him to cease gazing upon me, and his look was that of tender affection. At length, in a tone of deepest compassion and love, he said:

"'My dear Josephine, I have always loved you. I love you still. Do you still love me, excellent and good Josephine? Do you still love me, in spite of the relations I have again contracted, and which have separated me from you? But they have not banished you from my memory.'

" 'Sire,' I replied—

" 'Call me Bonaparte,' said he; 'speak to me, my beloved, with the same freedom, the same familiarity as ever.'

"Bonaparte soon disappeared, and I heard only the sound of his retiring footsteps. Oh, how quickly does everything take place on earth. I had once more felt the pleasure of being loved."

In reference to this melancholy event, Napoleon said, at Saint Helena:

"My divorce has no parallel in history. It did not destroy the ties which united our families, and our mutual tenderness remained unchanged. Our separation was a sacrifice, demanded of us by reason, for the interests of my crown and of my dynasty. Josephine was devoted to me. She loved me tenderly. No one ever had a preference over me in her heart. I occupied the first place in it, her children the next. She was right in thus loving me; and the remembrance of her is still all-powerful in my mind. Josephine was really an amiable woman: she was so kind, so humane. She was the best woman in France.

"A son, by Josephine, would have completed my happiness, not only in a political point of view, but as a source of domestic felicity. As a political result it would have secured to me the possession of the throne. The French people would have been as much attached to the son of Josephine as they were to the King of Rome, and I should not have set my foot on an abyss covered with a bed of flowers. But how vain are all human calculations! Who can pretend to decide on what may lead to happiness or unhappiness in this life!"

The divorce of Josephine, strong as were the political motives which led to it, was a violation of the immutable laws of God. Like all wrongdoing, however seemingly prosperous for a time, it promoted final disaster and woe. Doubtless Napoleon, educated in the midst of those convulsions which had shaken all the foundations of Christian morality, did not clearly perceive the extent of the wrong. He unquestionably felt that he was doing right; that the interests of France demanded the sacrifice. But the penalty was none the less inevitable. The laws of God cannot be violated with impunity, even though the violation be a sin of ignorance.

Chapter VI
The Death of Josephine

From the sad scenes described in the last chapter, Eugene returned to Italy. Hortense, in the deepest state of dejection, remained for a short time in Paris, often visiting her mother at Malmaison. About five months after the divorce, Napoleon was again married to Maria Louisa, daughter of the Emperor of Austria. The marriage ceremony was first celebrated with great pomp in Vienna, Napoleon being represented by proxy; and again the ceremony was repeated in Paris. It devolved upon Hortense, as the daughter of Napoleon, and the most prominent lady of his household, to receive with smiles of welcome and cordiality of greeting the princess who took the place of her mother. Seldom has it been the lot of a woman to pass through a more painful ordeal. Josephine, that she might be far removed from the tumult of Paris, rejoicing upon the arrival of Maria Louisa, retired from Malmaison to the more distant palace of Navarre. Soon after the marriage, Hortense hastened to join her mother there. There was at this time but little sympathy between Hortense and her husband. The power of a great sorrow in the death of their eldest son had for a short time brought them more closely together. There was, however, but little compatibility in their tastes and dispositions; and Hortense, deeming it her duty to comfort her mother, and finding more congeniality in her society than in that of her husband, made but brief visits to Holland.

It is easy for the prosperous and the happy to be amiable. Hortense was in a state of great physical debility, and almost every hope of her life had been crushed out. The letters of Hortense to Josephine have not been made public. We can only judge of their character from the replies which her mother made. From these it would appear that scarcely did a ray of joy illumine the gloomy path which she was destined to tread. On the 4th of April, 1810, Josephine wrote to Hortense from Navarre:

> "I am touched, my dear Hortense, with all the griefs which you experience. I hope that there is no more question of your

return to Holland, and that you will have a little repose. I know how much you must suffer from these disappointments, but I entreat you not to allow yourself to be affected by them. As long as anything remains to me you shall be mistress of your destiny; grief and happiness—you know that I share all with you.

"Take, then, a little courage, my dear daughter. We both of us have much need of it. Often mine is too feeble, and sorrow makes me sick. But I seek fortitude all the time, and with my utmost efforts."

Soon after this Hortense, taking her two children with her, rejoined her husband, King Louis, in Holland. Josephine wrote to her on the 10th of May, from Navarre:

"I have received your letter, my dear Hortense, and I see, with much pain, that your health is not good. I hope that repose will re-establish it; and I cannot doubt that the king will contribute to it everything in his power, by his attentions and his attachments. Every day will lead him to see more and more how much you merit. Take care of yourself, my dear daughter; you know how much I have need of you. My heart has suffered to a degree which has somewhat impaired my health. But fortitude triumphs over sorrow, and I begin to be a little better."

Again, on the 15th, the Empress wrote to Hortense, who was still in Amsterdam:

"I have been extremely anxious on account of your health, my dear Hortense. I know that you have experienced several attacks of fever, and I have need to be tranquilized.

"Your letter of the 10th has just reached me, but it has not given me the consolation I had hoped for. I see in it an abandonment of yourself, which gives me great pain. How many ties are there which should bind you to life! And if you have so little affection for me, is it then, when I am no longer happy, that you can think, with so much tranquility, of leaving me?

"Take courage, my daughter, and especially be careful of your health. I am confident, as I have already sent you word, that the waters which have been prescribed for you will do you good. Speak of it to the king with frankness. He certainly will not refuse you anything which may be essential to your health. I am making all my arrangements to go to the springs in the month of June. But I do not think that I shall go to Aix-la-Chapelle, but rather to Aix in Savoy, which place I prefer.

"Diversion of mind is necessary for my health, and I have more hope of finding that in a place which I have never seen, and whose situation is picturesque. The waters of Aix are particularly efficacious for the nerves. I earnestly recommend you to take them instead of those of Plombières. We can pass the time together. Reply to me immediately upon this subject. We can lodge together. It will not be necessary for you to take many companions with you. I shall take but very few, intending to travel incognito. Tomorrow I go to Malmaison, where I shall remain until I leave for the springs. I see with pleasure that the health of Louis Napoleon is good, and that he has not suffered from the change of air. Embrace him for me, my dear Hortense, and love me as tenderly as I love you.

"JOSEPHINE.

"P. S.—Remember me to the king."

For some unexplained reason, Hortense repaired first to the waters of Plombières. Her youngest son, Louis Napoleon, was sent to Malmaison, to be with Josephine, who so fondly loved the child that she was quite unwilling to be separated from him. Hortense took her elder child, Napoleon Louis, with her to the springs. Here she was taken very sick. On the 14th of June Josephine wrote her from Malmaison:

"I did not know how much you had suffered, my dear Hortense, until you were better; but I had a presentiment of it, and my anxiety induced me to write to one of your ladies, to indicate to her the telegraph from Nancy, as a prompt resource to call a physician. You ask me what I am doing. I had yesterday a day of happiness. The Emperor came to see me. His presence made me happy, although it renewed my grief. These are emotions such as one could wish often to experience.

"All the time he remained with me I had sufficient fortitude to restrain the tears which I felt were ready to flow. But after he had left, I had no longer power to restrain them, and I found myself very unhappy. He was kind to me, and amiable as ever; and I hope that he will have read in my heart all the affection and all the devotion with which I cherish him.

"I spoke to him of your situation, and he listened to me with interest. He is of opinion that you should not return to Holland, the king not having conducted as he would wish to have him. The opinion of the Emperor is that you should take the waters for the necessary time; that you should then write to your husband that it is the opinion of your physicians that you should reside in a warm climate for some time, and that consequently you are going to Italy. As to your son, the Emperor will give orders that he is not to leave France.

"I hope to see you, perhaps at Aix in Savoy, if the waters at Plombières do not agree with you; perhaps in Switzerland, where the Emperor has permitted me to journey. We shall be able to appoint for ourselves a rendezvous where we may meet. Then I will relate to you with the living voice those details which it would require too much time to write. I intend to leave next Monday for Aix in Savoy. I shall travel incognito, under the name of Madame d'Aubery. Your son (Louis Napoleon), who is now here, is very well. He has rosy cheeks and a fair skin."

Immediately upon Josephine's arrival at Aix, she wrote again to Hortense, who was still at Plombières, a letter expressive of great anxiety for her health and happiness, and entreating her to come and join her at Aix. "How I regret," she wrote, "not having known, before my departure, the true state of your health. I should have been at Plombières to take care of you, and I should not have experienced the anxiety which tortures me at this great distance. My only consolation is to think that you will soon come here. Let me soon see you. Alone, desolate, far from all my friends, and in the midst of strangers, you can judge how sad I am, and all the need I have of your presence."

In July, Louis Bonaparte abdicated the throne of Holland. Hortense wrote to her mother all the details of the event. Josephine engaged a cottage at Aix for herself and Hortense. She wrote to Hortense on the 18th of July:

> "I am delighted with the resolution you have taken to come here. I am occupied, in preparing your lodgings, more pleasantly than I could have hoped. A gentleman here has relinquished his house. I have accepted it, for it is delightfully situated, and the view is enchanting. The houses here are very small, but that which you will inhabit is larger. You can ride anywhere in a calèche. You will be very glad to have your own. I have mine, and I ride out in it every day. Adieu, my dear Hortense. I am impatient for the moment when I can embrace you."

As it was not deemed proper for the young princes, the sons of Hortense, to leave France, they were both left at the chateau of St. Cloud, while Hortense visited her mother at Aix. The devoted friend of Hortense, Madame Broc, to whom we have previously alluded, accompanied the ex-queen to Aix. The two friends frequently enjoyed long walks together in that region full of picturesque scenery. Hortense had a very keen appreciation of the beauties of nature, and had attained much excellence as a landscape painter. Aix, from its deep retirement and physical grandeur, became quite a favorite retreat. She had but little heart for any society but that of the solitudes of nature.

About the first of October Hortense returned, by the advice of the Emperor, to Fontainebleau, where she was reunited to her two sons. Josephine was, in the meantime, taking a short tour in Switzerland. We have previously spoken of Hortense's taste for music, and her skill as a composer. One of the airs, or *romances,* as they were called, composed by Hortense still retains in Europe perhaps unsurpassed popularity. It was termed familiarly *Beau Dunois,* or the Knight Errant. Its full title was *"Partant pour la Syrie, le jeune et beau Dunois."*[1]

---

[1] The writer remembers that forty years ago this was a favorite song in this country. At Bowdoin College it was the popular college song. It is now, in France, one of the favorite national airs.

Josephine, writing from Geneva to Hortense at Fontainebleau, says: "I have heard sung all over Switzerland your romance of Beau Dunois! I have even heard it played upon the piano with beautiful variations." Josephine soon returned to Navarre, which at that time she preferred to Malmaison, as it was farther removed from the capital, and from the tumult of joy with which the birth of the child of Maria Louisa would be received. On the 20th of March, 1811, all France resounded with acclamations at the birth of the young King of Rome. Hortense, devoting herself to her children, remained in Paris and its environs. In the autumn of this year Josephine left Navarre, and returned to Malmaison to spend the winter there. Hortense and her husband, though much estranged from each other, and living most of the time apart, were still not formally separated, and occasionally dwelt together. The ostensible cause of the frequent absence of Hortense from her husband was the state of her health, rendering it necessary for her to make frequent visits to the springs, and the griefs of her mother requiring often the solace of her daughter's presence.

Louis Bonaparte owned a very beautiful estate, called St. Leu, in France. Early in May, 1812, Napoleon left Paris for the fatal campaign to Moscow. Just before his departure, he called at Malmaison and took an affectionate leave of Josephine. Hortense was at St. Leu, with her children. After a short visit which Josephine made to St. Leu, and which she describes as delightful, she returned to Malmaison, and Hortense went to the springs of Aix-la-Chapelle, taking her two children with her. Here Napoleon Louis was attacked with scarlet fever, which caused his mother and the Empress great anxiety.

Josephine wrote to her, on the 28th of July: "You are very kind not to have forgotten me in the midst of your anxiety for your son. Embrace for me that dear child, and my little *Oui Oui*" (yes, yes).[1] Again she wrote, two days after: "I hope that our dear Napoleon continues to improve, and that the little *Oui Oui* is doing well." Eugene, leaving his amiable and much-loved wife and little family at Milan, had accompanied Napoleon on his Russian campaign. During his absence Josephine visited Milan, and there, as everywhere else, won the love of all who saw her. Hortense, with her children, was most of the time in Paris. Eugene, immediately after the terrible

---
[1]Oui Oui was the pet name given to little Louis Napoleon.

battle of Borodino, wrote as follows to Josephine. His letter was dated September 8, 1812.

> "MY GOOD MOTHER,—I write you from the field of battle. The Emperor has gained a great victory over the Russians. The battle lasted thirteen hours. I commanded the right, and hope that the Emperor will be satisfied.
>
> "I cannot sufficiently thank you for your attentions and kindness to my little family. You are adored at Milan, as everywhere else. They write me most charming accounts of you, and you have won the love of every one with whom you have become acquainted. Adieu! Please give tidings of me to my sister. I will write her tomorrow. Your affectionate son,
>
> "EUGENE."

The latter part of October of this year, 1812, Napoleon commenced his awful retreat from Moscow. Josephine and Hortense were much of the time together in a state of indescribable suspense and anguish. At midnight, on the 18th of December, Napoleon arrived in Paris. The disasters in Russia had caused a new coalition of all the dynasties against France. The Emperor of Austria, unmindful of the marriage of his daughter with Napoleon, had joined the coalition with all the military powers of his empire. The majestic army with which Napoleon had invaded Russia was almost annihilated, and nearly two millions of bayonets were now directed against the Republican Empire.

All France rose with enthusiasm to co-operate with Napoleon in his endeavors to resist the thronging foes. By the middle of April, nearly three hundred thousand men were on the march from France towards Germany, gallantly to meet the onswelling flood of more than a million of bayonets. On the 15th of April, 1813, at four o'clock in the morning, Napoleon left St. Cloud for the seat of war. The terrific campaign of Lutzen, Bautzen, Dresden, and Leipsic ensued.

Days of darkness were lowering around the Empire. The health of Hortense rendered it necessary for her to go to the springs of Aix in Savoy. Her two children were left with her mother at Malmaison. Under date of June 11, 1813, the Empress wrote to her daughter:

> "I have received your letter of the 7th, my dear Hortense. I see with pleasure that you have already been benefited by

the waters. I advise you to continue them, in taking, as you do, a few days of repose. Be very tranquil respecting your children. They are perfectly well. Their complexion is of the lily and the rose. I can assure you that since they have been here they have not had the slightest indisposition. I must relate to you a very pretty response on the part of *Oui Oui*. The Abbé Bertrand caused him to read a fable where there was a question about *metamorphosis*. Being called to explain the word, he said to the abbé:

" 'I wish I could change myself into a little bird, I would then fly away at the hour of your lesson; but I would return when M. Hase (his teacher of German) arrived.'

" 'But, prince,' remarked the abbé, 'it is not very polite for you to say that to me.' 'Oh,' replied *Oui Oui*, 'that which I say is only for the lesson, not for the man.'

"Do you not think, with me, that that repartee was very *spirituelle?* It was impossible for him to extricate himself from the embarrassment with more delicacy and gracefulness. Your children were with me when I received your letter. They were very happy to receive tidings from their mamma. Continue to write often, my dear daughter, for their sake and for mine. It is the only means to enable me to support your absence."

While upon this visit to Aix, Hortense was accompanied by her inseparable friend, Madame Broc. One day Hortense and Adèle were ascending a mountain, whose summit commanded a very magnificent view. Their path led over a deep, dark, craggy ravine, which was swept by a mountain torrent, foaming and roaring over the rocks. Alpine firs, casting a gloomy shade, clung to its sides. A frail rustic bridge crossed the chasm. Hortense with light step passed over in safety. Madame Broc followed. A piercing shriek was heard, followed by a crash. As Hortense turned round she saw that the bridge had given way, and her companion was falling, torn and mangled, from rock to rock, till the rushing torrent seized her and whirled her lifeless body down the gulf in its wild waters. There was no possibility of rescue. For a moment the fluttering robes of the unfortunate lady were seen in the midst of the surging flood, and then the body was swept away far down the dismal gorge.

The death of Madame Broc.

The shock which this frightful accident gave to the nerves of Hortense was like that which she experienced at the death of her son. For a time she seemed stunned by the blow, and reason tottered on its throne. Instead of flying from Aix, she lingered there. As soon as she partially recovered tranquility, she sought to divert her grief by entering the abodes of sickness, sorrow, and suffering in the neighborhood, administering relief with her own hands. She established a hospital at Aix from her own private funds for the indigent, and, like an angel of mercy, clothed the naked and fed the hungry, and, while her own heart was breaking, spoke words of consolation to the world-weary.

In reference to this event Josephine wrote from Malmaison to Hortense at Aix, under date of June 16, 1813:

> "What a horrible accident, my dear Hortense! What a friend you have lost, and by what a frightful calamity! Since yesterday, when I heard of it, I have been so horror-struck as not to be able to write to you. Every moment I have before my eyes the fate of that poor Adèle. Everybody is in tears for her. She was so beloved, so worthy of being beloved, by her excellent qualities and by her attachment for you. I can think of nothing but what condition you are in. I am so anxious, that I send my chamberlain, M. Turpin, to you, that he may give me more certain intelligence respecting your health. I shall make haste to leave myself for a short time, that my presence and my care may be useful to you. I feel keenly your grief. It is too well founded. But, my dear daughter, think of your children, who are so worthy of your love. Preserve yourself for them! Think also of your mother, who loves you tenderly.
>
> "JOSEPHINE."

Thus blow after blow fell upon the heart of poor Hortense. Two days after the above date Josephine wrote again, in reply to a letter from her daughter:

> "Your letter has reanimated me, my dear Hortense. In the dejection in which I was, I experienced true consolation in seeing your handwriting, and in being assured by yourself

that you try to conquer your grief. I fully realize how much it must cost you. Your letter, so tender, so touching, has renewed my tears. Ever since this frightful accident I have been sick. Alas! my dear daughter, you did not need this new trial.

"I have embraced your children for you. They also are deeply afflicted, and think of you very much. I am consoled in thinking that you will not forget us. I thank you for it, my dear Hortense, my daughter tenderly beloved."

Again, a few days after, this affectionate mother wrote to her grief-stricken child:

"I cannot permit your courier to leave without transmitting to you intelligence from me; without letting you know how much I think of you. I fear that you may surrender yourself too much to the grief which you have experienced. I shall not feel reassured until M. Turpin shall have returned. Think of your charming children, my dear Hortense. Think also of a mother who adores you, and whom your life alone attaches to the world. I hope that all these motives will give you courage to support with more resignation the loss of a friend so tender.

"I have just received a letter from Eugene. He fully shares your grief, and desires that you should go and pass some time with him, if you have sufficient strength. I should be happy to know that you were with him. Your children are enjoying perfect health. They are truly interesting. It would, indeed, touch your feelings if you knew how much they think of you. Life is very precious, and one clings to it when one has such good children. Adieu! my daughter. Think often of a mother who loves you tenderly, and who tenderly embraces you."

As nothing can more clearly reveal than do these confidential letters the character of Hortense, and the domestic relations of this illustrious and afflicted family, I insert them freely. They give us a rare view of, those griefs of our suffering humanity which are found in the palace no less than in the cottage. On the 29th of June, Josephine wrote again to Hortense:

"M. De Turpin has brought me your letter, my dear daughter. I see with pain how sad and melancholy you still are. But it is, at least, a great consolation to me to be assured that your health has not severely suffered. Take courage, my dear Hortense. I hope that happiness will yet be your lot. You have passed through many trials. Have not all persons their griefs? The only difference is in the greater or less fortitude of soul with which one supports them. That which ought particularly to soothe your grief is that everyone shares it with you. There are none who do not regret our poor Adèle as much for themselves as for you.

"Your children mourn over your sorrows. Everything announces in them an excellent character, and a strong attachment for you. The more I see of them the more I love them. Nevertheless, I do not spoil them. Feel easy on their account. We follow exactly what you have prescribed for their regimen and their studies. When they have done well during the week, I invite them to breakfast and dine with me on the Sabbath. The proof that they are in good health is that they have grown much. Napoleon had one eye slightly inflamed yesterday from the sting of a gnat. He was not, however, on that account, less well than usual. Today it is no longer manifest. It would not be worth mentioning, were we not in the habit of rendering you an exact account of everything which concerns them."

On the 6th of August Josephine wrote as follows:

"The beautiful days of summer have at last come with the month of August. I hope that they will strengthen you, my dear daughter. Your lungs will feel the influence of them, and the baths will do you much more good. I see with pleasure that you have not forgotten the years of your childhood, and you are very kind to your mother in recalling them to her. I did right in making happy, too, children so good and so affectionate, and they have since abundantly recompensed me for it. Your children will do the same for you, my dear Hortense. Their hearts resemble yours. They will never cease to love you. Their health is wonderfully good, and they have never been more fresh and vigorous.

"The little *Oui Oui* is always gallant and amiable to me. Two days ago, in seeing Madame Tascher leave us, who went to join her husband at the springs, he said to Madame Boucheporn:

" 'She must love her husband very much indeed, to be willing, for him, to leave my grandmother!'

"Do you not think that was charming? On the same day he went to walk in the woods of Butard. As soon as he was in the grand avenue, he threw his hat in the air, shouting, 'Oh, how I love beautiful nature!'[1]

"Not a day passes in which someone is not amused by his amiability. The children animate all around me. Judge if you have not rendered me happy in leaving them with me. I cannot be more happy until the day when I shall see you."

Disaster now followed disaster as the allied armies, in resistless numbers, crowded down upon France. The carnage of Dresden and Leipsic compelled the Emperor, in November, to return to Paris to raise reinforcements. Though he had been victorious in almost every battle, still the surging billows of his foes, flowing in upon him from all directions, could not be rolled back.

Maria Louisa was in a state of great embarrassment, and dreaded to see her husband. Her father, the Emperor of Austria, at the head of an immense army, was marching against France. When Napoleon, returning from the terrific strife, entered her apartment, Maria Louisa threw herself into his arms, and, unable to utter a word, burst into a flood of tears. Napoleon, having completed his arrangements for still maintaining the struggle, on the 25th of January, 1814, embraced his wife and child, and returned to the seat of war. He never saw wife or child again.

As his carriage left the door of the palace, the Emperor, pressing his forehead with his hand, said to Caulaincourt, who accompanied him, "I envy the lot of the meanest peasant of my empire. At my age he has discharged his debts to his country, and may remain at home enjoying the society of his wife and children, while I—I must fly to

[1] All will read with interest the above anecdotes of the childhood of Louis Napoleon, now Emperor of France. His manhood has more than fulfilled even the great promise of his early days. The stories which have been circulated in this country respecting his early dissipation are entirely unfounded. They originated in an error by which another Prince Bonaparte was mistaken for him.

the camp and engage in the strife of war. Such is the mandate of my inexplicable destiny."

After a moment's reverie, he added, "My good Louise is gentle and submissive. I can depend on her. Her love and fidelity will never fail me. In the current of events there may arise circumstances which will decide the fate of an empire. In that case I hope that the daughter of the Cæsars will be inspired by the spirit of her grandmother, Maria Theresa."

The struggle which ensued was short but awful. In the midst of these terrific scenes Napoleon kept up an almost daily correspondence with Josephine. On one occasion, when the surgings of the battle brought him within a few miles of Malmaison, he turned aside and sought a hurried interview with his most faithful friend. It was their last meeting. Napoleon took the hand of Josephine, and, gazing tenderly upon her, said:

"Josephine, I have been as fortunate as ever was man upon the face of this earth. But in this hour, when a storm is gathering over my head, I have not in this wide world anyone but you upon whom I can repose."

Soon after this, as the seat of war approached nearer to Paris, Josephine found it necessary to retire to Navarre. She wrote to Hortense, on the 28th of March: "Tomorrow I shall leave for Navarre. I have but sixteen men for a guard, and all wounded. I shall take care of them; but in truth I have no need of them. I am so unhappy in being separated from my children that I am indifferent respecting my fate."

At eight o'clock in the morning of the 29th Josephine took her carriage for Navarre. The Allies were rapidly approaching Paris, and a state of indescribable consternation filled the streets of the metropolis. Several times on the route the Empress was alarmed by the cry that the Cossacks were coming. The day was dark and stormy, and the rain fell in torrents. The pole of the carriage broke as the wheels sunk in a rut. Just at that moment a troop of horsemen appeared in the distance. The Empress, in her terror, supposing them to be the barbarous Cossacks, leaped from the carriage and fled through the fields. Was there ever a more cruel reverse of fortune? Josephine, the Empress of France, the admired of all Europe, in the frenzy of her alarm, rushing through the storm and the rain to seek refuge in the woods! The troops proved to be French. Her attendants followed and informed her of the mistake. She again entered her carriage, and uttered scarcely a word during the rest of her journey. Upon entering the palace of Navarre, she threw herself upon a couch, exclaiming:

"Surely Bonaparte is ignorant of what is passing within sight of the gates of Paris, or, if he knows, how cruel the thoughts which must now agitate his breast."

In a hurried letter which the Emperor wrote Josephine from Brienne, just after a desperate engagement with his vastly outnumbering foes, he said:

> "On beholding the scenes where I had passed my boyhood, and comparing my peaceful condition then with the agitation and terrors I now experience, I several times said, in my own mind, 'I have sought to meet death in many conflicts. I can no longer fear it. To me death would now be a blessing. But I would once more see Josephine.'"

Immediately after Josephine's arrival at Navarre, she wrote to Hortense, urging that she should join her at that place. In the letter she said:

> "I cannot tell you how sad I am. I have had fortitude in afflicted positions in which I have found myself, and I shall have enough to bear my reverses of fortune; but I have not sufficient to sustain me under absence from my children, and uncertainty respecting their fate. For two days I have not ceased to weep. Send me tidings respecting yourself and your children. If you can learn anything respecting Eugene and his family, inform me."

Two days after this, Hortense, with her two sons, joined her mother at Navarre. Paris was soon in the hands of the Allies. The Emperor Alexander invited Josephine and Hortense to return to Malmaison, where he established a guard for their protection. Soon after Napoleon abdicated at Fontainebleau. Upon the eve of his departure for Elba, he wrote to Josephine:

> "I wrote to you on the 8th. Possibly you have not received my letter. It may have been intercepted. At present

communications must be re-established. I have formed my resolution. I have no doubt that this billet will reach you. I will not repeat what I said to you. Then I lamented my situation. Now I congratulate myself thereon. My head and spirit are freed from an enormous weight. My fall is great, but at least is useful, as men say. Adieu! my dear Josephine. Be resigned as I am, and ever remember him who never forgets and never will forget you."

Josephine returned to Malmaison, and Hortense repaired to Rambouillet, to join Maria Louisa in these hours of perplexity and disaster. As soon as Maria Louisa set out under an Austrian escort for Vienna, Hortense rejoined her mother at Malmaison. Alexander was particularly attentive to Josephine and Hortense. He had loved Napoleon, and his sympathies were now deeply excited for his afflicted family. Through his kind offices, the beautiful estate of St. Leu, which Louis Bonaparte had owned, and which he had transferred to his wife, was erected into a duchy for her advantage, and the right of inheritance was vested in her children. The ex-Queen of Holland now took the title of the Duchess of St. Leu.

On the 10th of May the Emperor Alexander dined with Josephine at Malmaison. Grief, and a season unusually damp and cheerless, had seriously undermined her health. Notwithstanding acute bodily suffering, she exerted herself to the utmost to entertain her guests. At night she was worse and at times was delirious. Not long after this, Alexander and the King of Prussia were both guests to dine at Malmaison. The health of Josephine was such that she was urged by her friends not to leave her bed. She insisted, however, upon dressing to receive the allied sovereigns. Her sufferings increased, and she was obliged to retire, leaving Hortense to supply her place.

The next day Alexander kindly called to inquire for her health. Hour after hour she seemed to be slowly failing. On the morning of the 28th she fell into a lethargic sleep, which lasted for five hours, and her case was pronounced hopeless. Eugene and Hortense were at her side. The death-hour had come. The last rites of religion were administered to the dying. The Emperor Alexander was also in this chamber of grief. Josephine was perfectly rational. She called for the portrait of Napoleon, and, gazing upon it long and tenderly, breathed the following prayer:

"O God, watch over Napoleon while he remains in the desert of this world. Alas! though he hath committed great faults, hath he not expiated them by great sufferings? Just God, thou hast looked into his heart, and hast seen by how ardent a desire for useful and durable improvements he was animated. Deign to approve this my last petition, and may this image of my husband bear me witness that my latest wish and my latest prayer were for him and for my children."

Her last words were *"Island of Elba—Napoleon."* It was the 29th of May, 1814. For four days her body remained laid out in state, surrounded with numerous tapers. "Every road," writes a French historian, "from Paris and its environs to Ruel was crowded with trains of mourners. Sad groups thronged all the avenues; and I could distinguish tears even in the splendid equipages which came rattling across the courtyard."

More than twenty thousand persons—monarchs, nobles, statesmen, and weeping peasants—thronged the chateau of Malmaison to take the last look of the remains of one who had been universally beloved. The funeral took place at noon of the 2d of June. The remains were deposited in the little church of Ruel. A beautiful mausoleum of white marble, representing the Empress kneeling in her coronation robes, bears the simple inscription:

EUGENE AND HORTENSE
TO
JOSEPHINE.

Chapter VII
The Sorrows of Exile

There probably never was a more tender, loving mother than Josephine. And it is not possible that any children could be more intensely devoted to a parent than were Eugene and Hortense to their mother. The grief of these bereaved children was heartrending. Poor Hortense was led from the grave almost delirious with woe. Etiquette required that Eugene, passing through Paris, should pay his respects to Louis XVIII. The king had remarkable tact in paying compliments. Eugene announced himself simply as General Beauharnais. He thanked the king for the kind treatment extended by the allied monarchs to his mother and his sister. Hortense was also bound, by the laws of courtesy, to call upon the king in expression of gratitude. They were both received with so much cordiality as to expose the king to the accusation of having become a rank Bonapartist. On the other hand, Eugene and Hortense were censured by the partisan press for accepting any favors from the Allies. After the interview of Louis XVIII with Hortense, in which she thanked him for the Duchy of St. Leu, the king said to the Duke de Duras: "Never have I seen a woman uniting such grace to such distinguished manners; and I am a judge of women."

It is very difficult to ascertain with accuracy the movements of Hortense during the indescribable tumult of the next few succeeding months. The Duke of Rovigo says that Hortense reproached the Emperor Alexander for turning against Napoleon, for whom he formerly had manifested so much friendship. But the Emperor replied: "I was compelled to yield to the wishes of the Allies. As for myself personally, I wash my hands of everything which has been done."

The death of Josephine and the departure of Eugene left Hortense, bereaved and dejected, almost alone in Paris with her two children. Their intelligence and vivacity had deeply interested Alexander and other royal guests, who had cordially paid their tribute of respect and sympathy to their mother. Napoleon had taken a deep interest in the education of the two princes, as he was aware of the frailty of life, and as the death of the King of Rome would bring them in the direct line to the inheritance of the crown.

The Emperor generally breakfasted alone when at home, at a small table in his cabinet. The two sons of Hortense were frequently admitted, that they might interest him with their infant prattle. The Emperor would tell them a story, and have them repeat it after him, that he might ascertain the accuracy of their memory. Any indication of intellectual superiority excited in his mind the most lively satisfaction. Mademoiselle Cochelet, who was the companion and reader of Queen Hortense, relates the following anecdote of Louis Napoleon:

"The two princes were in intelligence quite in advance of their years. This proceeded from the care which their mother gave herself to form their characters and to develop their faculties. They were, however, too young to understand all the strange scenes which were transpiring around them. As they had always beheld in the members of their own family, in their uncles and aunts, kings and queens, when the Emperor of Russia and the King of Prussia were first introduced to them, the little Louis Napoleon asked if they were also their uncles, and if they were to be called so.

" 'No,' was the reply; 'they are not your uncles. You will simply address them as sire.'

" 'But are not all kings our uncles?' inquired the young prince.

" 'Far from being your uncle,' was the reply, 'they have come, in their turn, as conquerors.'

" 'Then they are the enemies,' said Louis Napoleon, 'of our uncle, the Emperor. Why, then, do they embrace us?'

" 'Because the Emperor of Russia, whom you see, is a generous enemy. He wishes to be useful to you and to your mamma. But for him you would no longer have anything; and the condition of your uncle, the Emperor, would be more unhappy.'

" 'We ought, then, to love this Emperor, ought we?'

" 'Yes, certainly,' was the reply; 'for you owe him your gratitude.'

"The next time the Emperor Alexander called upon Hortense, little Louis Napoleon, who was naturally very retiring and reticent, took a ring which his uncle Eugene had given him, and, stealing timidly over to Alexander, slipped the ring into his hand, and, half frightened, ran away with all speed. Hortense called the child to her, and asked him what he had done. Blushing deeply, the warm-hearted boy said:

" 'I have nothing but the ring. I wanted to give it to the Emperor, because he is good to my mamma.'

"Alexander cordially embraced the prince, and, putting the ring upon his watch chain, promised that he would always wear it."

The remains of Napoleon Charles, who had died in Holland, had been deposited, by direction of Napoleon, in the vaults of St. Denis, the ancient burial place of the kings of France. So great was the jealousy of the Bourbons of the name of Napoleon, and so unwilling were they to recognize in any way the right of the people to elect their own sovereign, that the government of Louis XVIII ordered the body to be immediately removed. Hortense transferred the remains of her child to the church of St. Leu.

Notwithstanding this jealousy, Alexander and the King of Prussia could not ignore the imperial character of Napoleon, whose government they had recognized, and with whom they had exchanged ambassadors and formed treaties: neither could they deny that the King of Holland had won a crown recognized by all Europe. They and the other crowned heads, who paid their respects to Hortense, in accordance with the etiquette of courts, invariably addressed each of the princes as *Your Royal Highness*. Hortense had not accustomed them to this homage. She had always addressed the eldest as Napoleon, the youngest as Louis. It was her endeavor to impress them with the idea that they could be nothing more than their characters entitled them to be. But after this, when the Bourbon Government assumed that Napoleon was an usurper, and that popular suffrage could give no validity to the crown, then did Hortense, in imitation of Napoleon at St. Helena, firmly resist the insolence. Then did she teach her children that they were princes, that they were entitled to the throne of France by the highest of all earthly authority—the almost unanimous voice of the French people—and that the Bourbons, trampling popular rights beneath their feet, and ascending the throne through the power of foreign bayonets, were usurpers.

Madame Cochelet, the reader of Queen Hortense, writes, in her interesting memoirs: "I have often seen her take her two boys on her knees, and talk with them in order to form their ideas. It was a curious conversation to listen to, in those days of the splendors of the empire, when those children were the heirs of so many crowns, which the Emperor was distributing to his brothers, his officers, his allies. Having questioned them on everything they knew already, she passed in review whatever they should know besides, if they were to rely upon their own resources for a livelihood.

" 'Suppose you had no money,' said Hortense to the eldest, 'and were alone in the world, what would you do, Napoleon, to support yourself?'

" 'I would become a soldier,' was the reply, 'and would fight so well that I should soon be made an officer.'

" 'And Louis,' she inquired of the younger, 'how would you provide for yourself?'

"The little prince, who was then but about five years old, had listened very thoughtfully to all that was said. Knowing that the gun and the knapsack were altogether beyond his strength, he replied:

" 'I would sell violet bouquets, like the little boy at the gate of the Tuileries, from whom we purchase them every day.' "

The boy is father of the man. Such has been Louis Napoleon from that hour to this; the quiet student—hating war, loving peace—all devoted to the arts of utility and of beauty. He has been the great pacificator of Europe. But for his unwearied efforts, the Continent would have been again and again in a blaze of war. As all present at this conversation smiled, in view of the unambitious projects of the prince, Hortense replied:

"This is one of my lessons. The misfortune of princes born on the throne is that they think everything is their due; that they are formed of a different nature from other men, and therefore never feel under any obligations to them. They are ignorant of human miseries, or think themselves beyond their reach. Thus, when misfortunes come, they are surprised, terrified, and always remain sunk below their destinies."

The Allies retired, with their conquering armies. Hortense remained with her children in Paris. Louis Bonaparte, sick and dejected, took up his residence in Italy. He demanded the children. A mother's love clung to them with tenacity which could not be relaxed. There was an appeal to the courts. Hortense employed the most eminent counsel to plead her cause. Eleven months passed away from the time of the abdication; and upon the very day when the court rendered its decision, that the father should have the eldest

Hortense and her children.

child, and the mother the youngest, Napoleon landed at Cannes, and commenced his almost miraculous march to Paris. The sublime transactions of the "One Hundred Days" caused all other events, for a time, to be forgotten.

Hortense was at the Tuileries, one of the first to greet the Emperor as he was borne in triumph, upon the shoulders of the people, up the grand staircase. "Sire," said Hortense, "I had a presentiment that you would return, and I waited for you here." The Allies had robbed the Emperor of his son, and the child was a prisoner with his mother in the palaces of Vienna. Very cordially Napoleon received his two nephews, and kept them continually near him. With characteristic devotion to the principle of universal suffrage, Napoleon submitted the question of his re-election to the throne of the empire to the French people. More than a million of votes over all other parties responded in the affirmative.

On the first of June, 1815, the Emperor was reinaugurated on the field of Mars, and the eagles were restored to the banners. It was one of the most imposing pageants Paris had ever witnessed. Hundreds of thousands crowded that magnificent parade ground. As the Emperor presented the eagles to the army, a roar as of reverberating thunder swept along the lines. By the side of the Emperor, upon the platform, sat his two young nephews. He presented them separately to the departments and the army as in the direct line of inheritance. This scene must have produced a profound impression upon the younger child, Louis Napoleon, who was so thoughtful, reflective, and pensive.

In the absence of Maria Louisa, who no longer had her liberty, Hortense presided at the Tuileries. Inheriting the spirit of her mother, she was unfailing in deeds of kindness to the many Royalists who were again ruined by the return of Napoleon. Her audience chamber was ever crowded by those who, through her, sought to obtain access to the ear of the Emperor. Napoleon was overwhelmed by too many public cares to give much personal attention to private interests.

The evening before Napoleon left his cabinet for his last campaign, which resulted in the disaster at Waterloo, he was in his cabinet conversing with Marshal Soult. The door was gently opened, and little Louis Napoleon crept silently into the apartment. His features were swollen with an expression of the profoundest grief, which he seemed to be struggling in vain to repress. Tremblingly he approached the Emperor, and, throwing himself upon his knees, buried his face in his two hands in the Emperor's lap, and burst into a flood of tears.

"What is the matter, Louis?" said the Emperor, kindly; "why do you interrupt me, and why do you weep so?"

The young prince was so overcome with emotion that for some time he could not utter a syllable. At last, in words interrupted by sobs, he said,

"Sire, my governess has told me that you are going away to the war. Oh! do not go! do not go!"

The Emperor, much moved, passed his fingers through the clustering ringlets of the child, and said, tenderly,

"My child, this is not the first time that I have been to the war. Why are you so afflicted? Do not fear for me. I shall soon come back again."

"Oh! my dear uncle," exclaimed the child, weeping convulsively; "those wicked Allies wish to kill you. Let me go with you, dear uncle, let me go with you!"

The Emperor made no reply, but, taking Louis Napoleon upon his knee, pressed him to his heart with much apparent emotion. Then calling Hortense, the mother of the child, he said to her:

"Take away my nephew, Hortense, and reprimand his governess, who, by her inconsiderate words, has so deeply excited his sympathies."

Then, after a few affectionate words addressed to the young prince, he was about to hand him to his mother, when he perceived that Marshal Soult was much moved by the scene.

"Embrace the child, Marshal," said the Emperor; "he has a warm heart and a noble soul. *Perhaps he is to be the hope of my race!*"

Napoleon returned from the disaster at Waterloo with all his hopes blighted. Hortense hastened to meet him, and to unite her fate with his. "It is my duty," she said. "The Emperor has always treated me as his child, and I will try, in return, to be his devoted and grateful daughter." In conversation with Hortense, Napoleon remarked: "Give myself up to Austria! Never. She has seized upon my wife and my son. Give myself up to Russia! That would be to a single man. But to give myself up to England, that would be to throw myself upon a *people.*" His friends assured him that, though he might rely upon the honor of the British *people,* he could not trust to the British *Government*. Hortense repaired to Malmaison with her two sons, where the Emperor soon rejoined her. "She restrained her own tears," writes Baron Fleury, "reminding us, with the wisdom of a philosopher and the sweetness of an angel, that we ought to surmount our sorrows and regrets, and submit with docility to the decrees of Providence."

It was necessary for Napoleon to come to a prompt decision. The Allies now nearly surrounded Paris. On the 29th of June the Emperor sat in his library at Malmaison, exhausted with care and grief. Hortense, though with swollen eyes and a heart throbbing with anguish, did everything which a daughter's love could suggest to minister to the solace of her afflicted father. Just before his departure to Rochefort, where he intended to embark for some foreign land, he called for his nephews, to take leave of them. It was a very affecting scene. Both of the children wept bitterly. The soul of the little, pensive Louis Napoleon was stirred to its utmost depths. He clung frantically to his uncle, screaming and insisting that he should go and "fire off the cannon!" It was necessary to take him away by force.

"The Emperor was departing almost without money. Hortense, after many entreaties, succeeded in making him accept her beautiful necklace, valued at eight hundred thousand francs. She sewed it up in a silk ribbon, which he concealed in his dress. He did not, however, find himself obliged to part with this jewel till on his deathbed, when he entrusted it to Count Montholon, with orders to restore it to Hortense. This devoted man acquitted himself successfully of this commission."[1]

Upon the departure of Napoleon, Hortense, with her children, returned to Paris. She was entreated by her friends to seek refuge in the interior of France, as the Royalists were much exasperated against her in consequence of her reception of the Emperor. They assured her that the army and the people would rally around her and her children as the representatives of the Empire. But Hortense replied:

"I must now undergo whatever fortune has in store for me. I am nothing now. I cannot pretend to make the people think that I rally the troops around me. If I had been Empress of France, I would have done everything to prolong the defense. But now it does not become me to mingle my destinies with such great interests, and I must be resigned."

---

[1] *Life of Napoleon III,* by Edward Roth.

In a few days the allied armies were again in possession of Paris. The Royalists assumed so threatening an attitude towards her, that she felt great solicitude for the safety of her children. Many persons kindly offered to give them shelter. But she was unwilling to compromise her friends by receiving from them such marks of attention. A kindhearted woman, by the name of Madame Tessier, kept a hose establishment on the Boulevard Montmartre. The children were entrusted to her care, where they would be concealed from observation, and where they would still be perfectly comfortable.

Hortense had her residence in a hotel on the Rue Cerutti. The Austrian Prince Schwartzenberg occupied the same hotel, and Hortense hoped that this circumstance would add to her security. But the Allies were now greatly exasperated against the French people, who had so cordially received the Emperor on his return from Elba. Even the Emperor Alexander treated Hortense with marked coldness. He called upon Prince Schwartzenberg without making any inquiries for her.

The hostility of the Allies towards this unfortunate lady was so great, that on the 19th of July Baron de Muffling, who commanded Paris for the Allies, received an order to notify the Duchess of St. Leu that she must leave Paris within two hours. An escort of troops was offered her, which amounted merely to an armed guard, to secure her departure and to mark her retreat. As Hortense left Paris for exile, she wrote a few hurried lines to a friend, in which she said:

"I have been obliged to quit Paris, having been positively expelled from it by the allied armies. So greatly am I, a feeble woman, with her two children, dreaded, that the enemy's troops are posted all along our route, as they say, to protect our passage, but in reality to insure our departure."

Prince Schwartzenberg, who felt much sympathy for Hortense, accompanied her, as a companion and a protector, on her journey to the frontiers of France. Little Louis Napoleon, though then but seven years of age, seemed fully to comprehend the disaster which had overwhelmed them, and that they were banished from their native land. With intelligence far above his years he conversed with his mother, and she found great difficulty in consoling him. It was through the influence of such terrible scenes as these that the character of that remarkable man has been formed.

It was nine o'clock in the evening when Hortense and her two little boys, accompanied by Prince Schwartzenberg, reached the

Hortense

Chateau de Bercy, where they passed the night. The next morning the journey was resumed towards the frontiers. It was the intention of Hortense to take refuge in a very retired country-seat which she owned at Pregny, in Switzerland, near Geneva. At some points on her journey the Royalists assailed her with reproaches. Again she was cheered by loudly-expressed manifestations of the sympathy and affection of the people. At Dijon the multitude crowding around her carriage, supposing that she was being conveyed into captivity, gallantly attempted a rescue. They were only appeased by the assurance of Hortense that she was under the protection of a friend.

Scarcely had this melancholy wanderer entered upon her residence at Pregny, with the title of the Duchess of St. Leu, ere the French minister in Switzerland commanded the Swiss government to issue an order expelling her from the Swiss territory. Switzerland could not safely disregard the mandate of the Bourbons of France, who were sustained in their enthronement by allied Europe. Thus pursued by the foes of the Empire, Hortense repaired to Aix, in Savoy. Here she met a cordial welcome. The people remembered her frequent visits to those celebrated springs, her multiplied charities, and here still stood, as an ever-during memorial of her kindness of heart, the hospital which she had founded and so munificently endowed. The magistrates at Aix formally invited her to remain at Aix so long as the Allied powers would allow her to make that place her residence.

It seemed as though Hortense were destined to drain the cup of sorrow to its dregs. Aix was the scene of the dreadful death of Madame Broc, which we have above described. Everything around her reminded her of that terrible calamity, and oppressed her spirits with the deepest gloom. And, to add unutterably to her anguish, an agent arrived at Aix from her husband, Louis Bonaparte, furnished with all competent legal powers to take custody of the eldest child and convey him to his father in Italy. It will be remembered that the court had decided that the father should have the eldest and the mother the youngest child. The stormy events of the "Hundred Days" had interrupted all proceedings upon this matter.

This separation was a terrible trial not only to the mother, but to the two boys. The peculiarities of their dispositions and temperaments fitted them to assimilate admirably together. Napoleon Louis, the elder, was bold, resolute, high-spirited. Louis Napoleon, the younger, was gentle, thoughtful, and pensive. The parting was very affecting—Louis Napoleon throwing his arms around his elder brother, and weeping as though his heart would break. The thoughtful child, thus companionless, now turned to his mother with the full flow of his affectionate nature. A French writer, speaking of these scenes, says:

"The soul of Hortense had been already steeped in misfortune, but her power of endurance seemed at length exhausted. When she had embraced her son for the last time, and beheld the carriage depart which bore him away, a deep despondency overwhelmed her spirits. Her very existence became a dream; and it seemed a matter of indifference to her whether her lot was to enjoy or to suffer, to be persecuted, respected, or forgotten."

And now came another blow upon the bewildered brain and throbbing heart of Hortense. The Allies did not deem it safe to allow Hortense and her child to reside so near the frontiers of France. They knew that the French people detested the Bourbons. They knew that all France, upon the first favorable opportunity, would rise in the attempt to re-establish the Empire. The Sardinian government was accordingly ordered to expel Hortense from Savoy. Where should she go? It seemed as though all Europe would refuse a home to this bereaved, heartbroken lady and her child. She remembered her cousin, Stephanie Beauharnais, her schoolmate, whom her mother and Napoleon had so kindly sheltered and provided for in the days when the Royalists were in exile. Stephanie was the lady to whom her father had been so tenderly attached. She was now in prosperity and power, the wife of the Grand Duke of Baden. Hortense decided to seek a residence at Constance, in the territory of Baden, persuaded that the duke and duchess would not drive her, homeless and friendless, from their soil, out again into the stormy world.

To reach Baden it was necessary to pass through Switzerland. The Swiss government, awed by France, at first refused to give her permission to traverse their territory. But the Duke of Richelieu intervened in her favor, and, by remonstrating against such cruelty, obtained the necessary passport. It was now the month of November. Cold storms swept the snow-clad hills and the valleys. Hortense departed from Aix, taking with her her son Louis Napoleon, his private tutor, the Abbé Bertrand, her reader, Mademoiselle Cochelet, and an attendant. She wished to spend the first night at her own house, at Pregny; but even this slight gratification was forbidden her.

The police were instructed to watch her carefully all the way. At Morat she was even arrested, and detained a prisoner two days, until instructions should be received from the distant authorities. At last she reached the city of Constance. But even here she found that her sorrows had not yet terminated. Neither the Duke of Baden nor the Duchess ventured to welcome her. On the contrary, immediately upon her arrival, she received an official notification that, however anxious the grand duke and duchess might be to afford her hospitable shelter, they were under the control of higher powers, and they must therefore request her to leave the duchy without delay. It was now intimated that the only countries in Europe which would be allowed to afford her a shelter were Austria, Prussia, or Russia.

The storms of winter were sweeping those northern latitudes. The health of Hortense was extremely frail. She was fatherless and motherless, alienated from her husband, bereaved of one of her children, and all her family friends dispersed by the ban of exile. She had no kind friends to consult, and she knew not which way to turn. Thus distracted and crushed, she wrote an imploring letter to her cousins, the Duke and Duchess of Baden, stating the feeble condition of her health, the inclement weather, her utter friendlessness, and exhaustion from fatigue and sorrow, and begging permission to remain in Constance until the ensuing spring.

In reply she received a private letter from the grand duchess, her cousin Stephanie, assuring her of her sympathy, and of the cordiality with which she would openly receive and welcome her, if she did but dare to do so. In conclusion, the duchess wrote: "Have patience, and do not be uneasy. Perhaps all will be right by spring. By that time passions will be calmed, and many things will have been forgotten."

Though this letter did not give any positive permission to remain, it seemed at least to imply that soldiers would not be sent to transport her, by violence, out of the territory. Somewhat cheered by this assurance, she rented a small house, in a very retired situation upon the western shore of the Lake of Constance. Though in the disasters of the times she had lost much property, she still had an ample competence. Her beloved brother, Eugene, it will be remembered, had married a daughter of the King of Bavaria. He was one of the noblest of men and the best of brothers. As soon as possible, he took up his residence near his sister. He also was in the enjoyment of an ample fortune. Thus there seemed to be for a short time a lull in those angry storms which for so long had risen dark over the way of Hortense.

In this distant and secluded home, upon the borders of the lake, Hortense and her small harmonious household passed the winter of 1815. Though she mourned over the absence of her elder child, little Louis Napoleon cheered her by his bright intelligence and his intense affectionateness. Prince Eugene often visited his sister; and many of the illustrious generals and civilians, who during the glories of the Empire had filled Europe with their renown, were allured as occasional guests to the home of this lovely woman, who had shared with them in the favors and the rebuffs of fortune.

Hortense devoted herself assiduously to the education of her son. She understood thoroughly the political position of France. Foreigners, with immense armies, had invaded the kingdom, and forced upon the reluctant people a detested dynasty. Napoleon was Emperor by popular election. The people still, with almost entire unanimity, desired the Empire. And Hortense knew full well that, so soon as the French people could get strength to break the chains with which foreign armies had bound them, they would again drive out the Bourbons and re-establish the Empire.

Hortense consequently never allowed her son to forget the name he bore, or the political principles which his uncle, the Emperor, had borne upon his banners throughout Europe. The subsequent life of this child has proved how deep was the impression produced upon his mind, as pensively, silently he listened to the conversation of the statesmen and the generals who often visited his mother's parlor. Lady Blessington about this time visited Hortense, and she gives the following account of the impression which the visit produced upon her mind:

"Though prepared to meet in Hortense Bonaparte, ex-Queen of Holland, a woman possessed of no ordinary powers of captivation, she has, I confess, far exceeded my expectations. I have seen her frequently, and spent two hours yesterday in her society. Never did time fly away with greater rapidity than while listening to her conversation, and hearing her sing those charming little French *romances*, written and composed by herself, which, though I had often admired them, never previously struck me as being so expressive and graceful as they now proved to be.

"I know not that I ever encountered a person with so fine a tact or so quick an apprehension as the Duchess of St. Leu. These give her the power of rapidly forming an appreciation of those with whom she comes in contact, and of suiting the subjects of conversation to their tastes and comprehensions. Thus, with the grave she is serious, with the lively gay, and with the scientific she only permits just a sufficient extent of her *savoir* to be revealed to encourage the development of theirs.

"She is, in fact, all things to all men, without losing a single portion of her own natural character; a peculiarity of which seems to be the desire, as well as the power, of sending all away who approach her satisfied with themselves and delighted with her. Yet there is no unworthy concession of opinions made, or tacit acquiescence yielded, to conciliate popularity. She assents to or dissents from the sentiments of others with a mildness and good sense which gratifies those with whom she coincides, or disarms those from whom she differs."

Chapter VIII
Peaceful Days, yet Sad

As the spring of the year 1816 opened upon Europe, Hortense was found residing undisturbed, with her son, Louis Napoleon, in their secluded home upon the shores of Lake Constance. The Allies seemed no longer disposed to disturb her. Still, she had many indications that she was narrowly watched. She was much cheered by a visit which she made to her brother at Berg, on the Wurmsee, where she was received with that warmth of affection which her wounded heart so deeply craved. Her health being still very frail, she, by the advice of her physicians, spent the heat of summer at the baths of Geiss, among the mountains of Appenzell. Her son, Louis Napoleon, was constantly with her. Nearly the whole attention of the mother was devoted to his education.

She had the general superintendence of all his studies, teaching him herself drawing and dancing, often listening to his recitations and guiding his reading. Her own highly-cultivated mind enabled her to do this to great advantage. The young prince read aloud to his mother in the evenings, the selections being regulated in accordance with his studies in geography or history. Saturday Hortense devoted the entire day to her son, reviewing all the reading and studies of the week. In addition to the Abbé Bertrand, another teacher was employed, M. Lebas, a young professor of much distinction from the Normal School of Paris.

Thus the summer and autumn of 1816 passed tranquilly away. But the eagle eye of the Bourbons was continually upon Hortense. They watched every movement she made, she could not leave her home, or receive a visit from any distinguished stranger, without exciting their alarm. Their uneasiness at length became so great that, early in the year 1817, the Duke of Baden received peremptory orders that he must immediately expel Hortense and her child from his territory. The Bourbons could not allow such dangerous personages to dwell so near the frontiers of France. Hortense was a feeble, heartbroken woman. Her child was but eight years of age. But they were representatives of the Empire. And the Bourbons were ever terror-stricken lest the French people should rise in insurrection, and demand the restoration of that Empire, of which foreign armies had robbed them.

In the extreme northeastern portion of Switzerland, on the southern shores of the Lake of Constance, there was the small Swiss canton of Thurgovia. The gallant magistrates of the canton informed Hortense that if she wished to establish herself in their country, she should be protected by both the magistrates and the people. The ex-queen had occasionally entered the canton in her drives, and had observed with admiration a modest but very beautiful chateau called Arenemberg, very picturesquely located on the borders of the lake. She purchased the estate for about sixty thousand francs. This became a very delightful summer residence, though in winter it presented a bleak exposure, swept by piercing winds. Until the death of Hortense, Arenemberg continued to be her favorite place of residence.

To add to this transient gleam of happiness, there was now a partial reconciliation between Hortense and her husband; and, to the unspeakable joy of the mother and Louis Napoleon, they enjoyed a visit of several months from Napoleon Louis. It is not easy to imagine the happiness which this reunion created, after a separation of nearly three years.

The judicious mother now thought it important that her sons should enjoy the advantages of a more public education than that which they had been receiving from private tutors at home. She accordingly took them both to Augsburg, in Bavaria, where they entered the celebrated college of that city. Hortense engaged a handsome residence there, that she might still be with her sons, whom she loved so tenderly. A French gentleman of distinction, traveling in that region, had the honor of an introduction to her, and gives the following account of his visit:

"Returning to France in 1819, after a long residence in Russia, I stopped at Augsburg, where the Duchess of St. Leu was then a resident. I had hitherto only known her by report. Some Russian officers, who had accompanied the Emperor Alexander to Malmaison in 1814, had spoken to me of Hortense with so much enthusiasm, that for the first few moments it appeared as if I saw her again after a long absence, and as if I owed my kind reception to the ties of ancient friendship. Everything about her is in exact harmony with the angelic expression of her face, her conversation, demeanor, and the sweetness of her voice and disposition.

"When she speaks of an affecting incident, the language becomes more touching through the depths of her sensibility. She lends so much life to every scene, that the auditor becomes witness of the transaction. Her powers of instructing and delighting are almost magical; and her artless fascination leaves on every heart those deep traces which even time can never efface.

"She introduced me to her private circle, which consisted of the two children and their tutors, some old officers of her household, two female friends of her infancy, and that living monument of conjugal devotion, Count Lavallette.[1] The conversation soon became general. They questioned me about the Ukraine, where I long had resided, and Greece and Turkey, through which I had lately traveled.

"In return, they spoke of Bavaria, St. Leu, the Lake of Constance, and, by degrees, of events deriving their chief interest from the important parts played by the narrators themselves. We dined at five. I afterwards accompanied the duchess into the garden, and, in the few moments then enjoyed of intimate conversation, I saw that no past praises had ever been exaggerated. How admirable were her feelings when she recalled the death of her mother, and in her tragic recital of the death of Madame Broc.

"But when she spoke of her children, her friends, and the fine arts, her whole figure seemed to glow with the ardor of her imagination. Goodness of heart was displayed in every feature, and gave additional value to her other estimable qualities. In describing her present situation it was impossible to avoid mentioning her beloved France.

" 'You are returning,' said she, 'to your native country;' and the last word was pronounced with a heartfelt sigh. I had been an exile from my cradle, yet my own eager anxiety to revisit a birthplace scarcely remembered, enabled me to estimate her grief at the thoughts of an eternal separation. She spoke of the measures adopted for her

---

[1] Count Lavallette was one of the devoted friends of Napoleon, who had long served in the armies of the Empire. For the welcome he gave Napoleon on his return from Elba he was doomed, by the Bourbons, to death. While preparations were being made for his execution, his wife and daughter, with her governess, were permitted to visit him. Very adroitly he escaped in his wife's clothes, she remaining in his place. Irritated by this escape, the Government held his wife a prisoner until she became a confirmed lunatic.

banishment with that true resignation which mourns but never murmurs. After two hours of similar conversation, it was impossible to decide which was the most admirable, her heart, her good sense, or her imagination.

"We returned to the drawing room at eight, where tea was served. The duchess observed that this was a habit learned in Holland, 'though you are not to suppose,' she added, with a slight blush, 'that it is preserved as a remembrance of days so brilliant, but now already so distant. Tea is the drink of cold climates, and I have scarcely changed my temperature.'

"Numerous visitors came from the neighborhood, and some even from Munich. She may, indeed, regard this attention with a feeling of proud gratification. It is based upon esteem alone, and is far more honorable than the tiresome adulation of sycophants while at St. Cloud or The Hague. In the course of the evening we looked through a suite of rooms containing, besides a few masterpieces of the different schools, a large collection of precious curiosities. Many of these elegant trifles had once belonged to her mother; and nearly everyone was associated with the remembrance of some distinguished personage or celebrated event. Indeed, her museum might almost be called an abridgment of contemporary history. Music was the next amusement; and the duchess sang, accompanying herself with the same correct taste which inspires her compositions. She had just finished the series of drawings intended to illustrate her collection of *romances*. How could I avoid praising that happy talent which thus personifies thought? The next day I received that beautiful collection as a remembrance.

"I took my leave at midnight, perhaps without even the hope of another meeting. I left her as the traveler parts from the flowers of the desert, to which he can never hope to return. But, wherever time, accident, or destiny may place me, the remembrance of that day will remain indelibly imprinted alike on my memory and heart. It is pleasing to pay homage to the fallen greatness of one like Hortense, who joins the rare gift of talents to the charms of the tenderest sensibility."

The residence of Hortense in Augsburg was in a mansion, since called Pappenheim Palace, in Holy Cross Street. After the graduation of her children, Hortense, with Louis Napoleon, spent most of their time at Arenemberg, interspersed with visits to Rome and Florence.

Hortense at Arenemberg.

Hortense

The beautiful chateau was situated upon a swell of land, with green lawns and a thick growth of forest trees, through which there were enchanting views of the mountain and of the lake. The spacious grounds were embellished with the highest artistic skill, with terraces, trellis-work woodbines, and rare exotics.

"The views," writes an English visitor, "which were in some places afforded through the woods, and in others, by their rapid descent, carried over them, were broken in a manner which represented them doubly beautiful. From one peep you caught the small vine-clad island of Reichman, with its cottage gleams trembling upon the twilighted lake. From another you had a noble reach of the Rhine, going forth from its brief resting-place to battle its way down the Falls of Schaffhausen; and beyond it the eye reposed upon the distant outline of the Black Forest, melting warmly in the west. In a third direction you saw the vapory steeples of Constance, apparently sinking in the waters which almost surrounded them; and far away you distinguish the little coast villages, like fading constellations, glimmering fainter and fainter, till land and lake and sky were blended together in obscurity."

Not far distant was the imposing chateau of Wolfberg, which had been purchased by General Parguin, a young French officer of the Empire of much distinction. He had married Mademoiselle Cochelet, and became one of the most intimate friends of Louis Napoleon.

Prince Eugene had also built him a house in the vicinity, that he might be near his sister and share her solitude. Just as the house was finished, and before he moved into it, Eugene died. This was another crushing blow to the heart of Hortense. She was in Rome at the time, and we shall have occasion to refer to the event again.

Hortense, in her retirement, was no less a queen than when the diadem was upon her brow. Though at the farthest possible remove from all aristocratic pride, her superior mind, her extraordinary attainments, and her queenly grace and dignity, invested her with no less influence over the hearts of her friends than she enjoyed in her days of regal power. A visitor at Wolfberg, in the following language, describes a call which Hortense made upon Madame Parguin and her guests at the chateau:

"One fine evening, as we were all distributed about the lawn at Wolfberg, there was an alarm that Hortense was coming to visit Madame Parguin. As I saw her winding slowly up the hill, with all her company, in three little summer carriages, the elegance of the cavalcade, in scenes where elegance was so rare, was exceedingly striking.

"The appearance of Hortense was such as could not fail to excite admiration and kind feeling. Her countenance was full of talent, blended with the mild expression of a perfect gentlewoman. Her figure, though not beyond the middle height, was of a mold altogether majestic. She lamented that she had not sooner known of the purposed length of our stay in that part of Switzerland, as, having conceived that we were merely passing a few days, she had been unwilling to occupy our time. She then spoke of her regret at not being able to entertain us according to her wishes. And, finally, she told us that she had in agitation some little theatricals which, if we could bear with such trifles, we should do her pleasure in attending. All this was said with simple and winning eloquence."

The room for this little theatric entertainment was in a small building, beautifully decorated, near the house. Many distinguished guests were present; many from Constance; so that the apartment was crowded to its utmost capacity. There were two short plays enacted. In one Hortense took a leading part in scenes of trial and sorrow, in which her peculiar powers were admirably displayed. Even making all suitable allowance for the politeness due from guests to their host, it is evident that Hortense possessed dramatic talent of a very high order.

From the theater the guests returned to the chateau, where preparations had been made for dancing. In the intervals between the dances there was singing, accompanied by the piano. "Here, again," writes one of the guests, "Hortense was perfectly at home. She sang several songs, of which I afterwards found her to be the unacknowledged composer. Among these was the beautiful air, *Partant pour la Syrie,* which will be a fair guaranty that I do not say too much for the rest."

At the close of the evening, as the guests began to depart, the remainder were dispersed through the suite of rooms, admiring the various objects of curiosity and of beauty with which they are decorated. There were some beautiful paintings, and several pieces of exquisite statuary. Upon the tables there were engravings, drawing-books, and works of *belles-lettres.*

"I chanced," writes the visitor from whom we have above quoted, "to place my hand upon a splendid album, and had the further good

Hortense

fortune to seat myself beside a beautiful young *dame de compagnie* of the duchess, who gave me the history of all the treasures I found therein. Whatever I found most remarkable was still the work of Hortense. Of a series of small portraits, sketched by her in colors, the likeness of those of which I had seen the subjects would have struck me, though turned upside down. She had the same power and the same affectionate feeling for fixing the remembrance of places likewise.

"The landscapes which she had loved in forbidden France, even the apartments which she had inhabited, were executed in a manner that put to shame the best amateur performances I had ever seen. There was a minute attention to fidelity in them, too, which a recollection of her present circumstances could not fail to bring home to the spectator's heart.

"I know not when my interest would have cooled in this mansion of taste and talent. Towards morning I was obliged to take my leave; and I doubt if there were any individual who returned home by that bright moonlight, without feeling that Hortense had been born some century and a half too late. For an age of bigots and turncoats she, indeed, seemed unsuited. In that of true poetry and trusty cavaliers, she would have been the subject of the best rhymes and rencontres in romantic France.

"After this I saw her frequently, both at her own house and at Wolfberg, and I never found anything to destroy the impression which I received on my introduction. Independently of the interest attached to herself, she had always in her company some person who had made a noise in the world, and had become an object of curiosity. At one time it was a distinguished painter or poet; again, it was a battered soldier, who preferred resting in retirement to the imputation of changing his politics for advancement; then a grand duke or duchess who had undergone as many vicissitudes as herself; and, finally, the widow of the unfortunate Marshal Ney.

"There was something in the last of these characters, particularly when associated with Hortense, more interesting than all the others. She was a handsome, but grave and silent woman, and still clad in mourning for her husband, whose death, so connected with the banishment of the duchess, could not fail to render them deeply sympathetic in each other's fortunes. The amusements provided for all this company consisted of such as I have mentioned—expeditions

Peaceful Days, yet Sad

to various beautiful spots in the neighborhood, and music parties on the water. The last of these used sometimes to have a peculiarly romantic effect; for on *fête* days the young peasant girls, all glittering in their golden tinsel bonnets, would push off with their sweethearts, like mad things, in whatever boats they could find upon the beach. I have seen them paddling their little fleet round the duchess's boat with all the curiosity of savages round a man-of-war.

"At length the time arrived for me to bid adieu to Switzerland. It was arranged that I should set out for Italy with a small party of my Wolfberg friends. An evening or two before we departed we paid a leave-taking visit to the duchess. She expressed much polite regret at our intention, and gave us a cordial invitation to renew our acquaintance with her in the winter at Rome. Her care, indeed, to leave a good impression of her friendly disposition upon our minds, was exceedingly gratifying. She professed to take an interest in the plans which each of us had formed, and, when her experience qualified her, gave us instructions for our travels.

"When we rose to depart, the night being fine, she volunteered to walk part of the way home with us. She came about a quarter of a mile to where she could command an uninterrupted view of the lake, above which the moon was just then rising, a huge red orb which shot a burning column to her feet. 'I will now bid you adieu,' she said; and we left her to the calm contemplation of grandeur which could not fade, and enjoyments which could not betray. This was the last time I saw, and perhaps shall ever see Hortense; but I shall always remember my brief acquaintance with her as a dip into days which gave her country the character of being the most polished of nations."

Hortense, with her son Louis Napoleon, had been in the habit of passing the severity of the winter months in the cities of Augsburg or Munich, spending about eight months of the year at Arenemberg. But after the death of her brother Eugene, the associations which those cities recalled were so painful that she transferred her winter residence to Rome or Florence. An English lady who visited her at Arenemberg writes:

"The style of living of the Duchess of St. Leu is sumptuous, without that freezing etiquette so commonly met with in the great. Her household still call her *Queen,* and her son *Prince* Napoleon or *Prince* Louis. The suite is composed of two ladies of honor, an equerry, and the tutor of her younger son. She has a numerous train of domestics, and it is among them that the traces are still observable of bygone pretensions, long since abandoned by the true nobleness of their mistress. The former queen, the daughter of Napoleon, the mother of the Imperial heir-apparent, has returned quietly to private life with the perfect grace of a voluntary sacrifice.

"The duchess receives strangers with inexpressible kindness. Ever amiable and obliging, she is endowed with that charming simplicity which inspires, at first sight, the confidence of intimate affection. She speaks freely of the brilliant days of her prosperity. And history then flows so naturally from her lips, that more may be learned as a delighted listener, than from all the false or exaggerated works so abundant everywhere. The deposed queen considers past events from such an eminence that nothing can interpose itself between her and the truth. This strict impartiality gives birth to that true greatness, which is a thousand times preferable to all the splendors she lost in the flower of her age.

"I have been admitted to the intimacy of the Duchess of St. Leu, both at Rome and in the country. I have seen her roused to enthusiasm by the beauties of nature, and have seen her surrounded by the pomp of ceremony; but I have never known her less than herself; nor has the interest first inspired by her character ever been diminished by an undignified sentiment or the slightest selfish reflection.

"It is impossible to be a more ardent and tasteful admirer of the fine arts than is the duchess. Everyone has heard her beautiful *romances*, which are rendered still more touching by the soft and melodious voice of the composer. She usually sings standing; and, although a finished performer on the harp and piano, she prefers the accompaniment of one of her attendant ladies. Many of her leisure hours are employed in painting. Miniatures, landscapes, and flowers are equally the subjects of her pencil. She declaims well, is a delightful player in comedy, acts proverbs with uncommon excellence, and I really know no one who can surpass her in every kind of needlework.

"The Duchess of St. Leu never was a regular beauty, but she is still a charming woman. She has the softest and most expressive blue eyes in the world. Her light flaxen hair contrasts beautifully with the dark color of her long eyelashes and eyebrows. Her complexion is fresh and of an even tint; her figure elegantly molded; her hands and feet perfect. In fine, her whole appearance is captivating in the extreme.

She speaks quickly with rapid gestures, and all her movements are easy and graceful. Her style of dress is rich, though she has parted with most of her jewels and precious stones."

Hortense was almost invariably accompanied by her son, Louis Napoleon, whether residing in Italy or in Switzerland. When at Arenemberg, the young prince availed himself of the vicinity to the city in pursuing a rigorous course of study in physics and chemistry under the guidance of a very distinguished French philosopher. He also connected himself, in prosecuting his military studies, with a Baden regiment garrisoned at Constance. He was here recognized as the Duke of St. Leu, and was always received with much distinction. At Rome, the residence of Hortense was the center of the most brilliant and polished society of the city. Here her son was introduced to the most distinguished men from all lands, and especially to the old friends of the Empire, who kept alive in his mind the memory of the brilliant exploits of him whose name he bore. Pauline Bonaparte, who had married for her second husband Prince Borghese, and who was immensely wealthy, also resided in the vicinity of Rome, in probably the most magnificent villa in Europe. Hortense and her son were constant visitors at her residence.

Madame Récamier, who had ever been the warm friend of the Bourbons, and whom Hortense had befriended when the Bourbons were in exile, gives the following account of an interview she had with Queen Hortense in Rome, early in the year 1824. The two friends had not met since the "Hundred Days" in 1815. We give the narrative in the words of Madame Récamier:

"I went one day to St. Peter's to listen to the music, so beautiful under the vaults of that immense edifice. There, leaning against a pillar, meditating under my veil, I followed with heart and soul the solemn notes that died away in the depths of the dome. An elegant-looking woman, veiled like myself, came and placed herself near the same pillar. Every time that a more lively feeling drew from me an involuntary movement my eyes met those of the stranger. She seemed to be trying to recognize my features. And I, on my side, through the obstacle of our veils, thought I distinguished blue eyes and light hair that were not unknown to me. 'Madame Récamier!' 'Is it you, madame?' we said almost at the same moment. 'How delighted I am to see you!' said Queen Hortense, for she it was. 'You know,' she added, smiling, 'that I would not have waited until now to find you out; but you have always been ceremonious with me.'

" 'Then, madame,' I replied, 'my friends were exiled and unfortunate. You were happy and brilliant, and my place was not near you.'

" 'If misfortune has the privilege of attracting you,' replied the queen, 'you must confess that my time has come and permit me to advance my claims.'

"I was a little embarrassed for a reply. My connection with the Duke de Laval, our ambassador at Rome, and with the French Government in general, was a barrier to any visiting between us. She understood my silence.

" 'I know,' she said, sadly, 'that the inconveniences of greatness follow us still, when even our prerogatives are gone. Thus, with loss of rank, I have not acquired liberty of action. I cannot today even taste the pleasures of a woman's friendship, and peaceably enjoy society that is pleasant and dear to me.'

"I bowed my head with emotion, expressing my sympathy only by my looks.

" 'But I must talk to you,' said the queen, more warmly. 'I have so many things to say to you. If we cannot visit each other, nothing prevents us from meeting elsewhere. We will appoint some place to meet. That will be charming.'

" 'Charming indeed, madame,' I replied, smiling; 'and especially for me. But how shall we fix the time and place for these interviews?'

" 'It is you,' Hortense replied, 'who must arrange that; for, thanks to the solitude forced upon me, my time is entirely at my own disposal. But it may not be the same with you. Sought for as you are, you mix, no doubt, a great deal in society.'

" 'Heaven forbid!' I replied. 'On the contrary, I lead a very retired life. It would be absurd to come to Rome to see society, and people everywhere the same. I prefer to visit what is peculiarly her own—her monuments and ruins.'

" 'Well, then, we can arrange everything finely,' added Hortense; 'if it is agreeable to you I will join you in these excursions. Let me know each day your plans for the next; and we will meet, as if by accident, at the appointed places.'

"I eagerly accepted this offer, anticipating much pleasure in making the tour of old Rome with so gracious and agreeable a companion, and one who loved and understood art. The queen, on her side, was happy in the thought that I would talk to her of France; whilst to both of us the little air of mystery thrown over these interviews gave them another charm.

" 'Where do you propose to go tomorrow?' asked the queen.

" 'To the Coliseum.'

" 'You will assuredly find me there,' Hortense replied. 'I have much to say to you. I wish to justify myself in your eyes from an imputation that distresses me.'

"The queen began to enter into explanations; and the interview threatening to be a long one, I frankly reminded her that the French ambassador, who had brought me to St. Peter's, was coming back for me; for I feared that a meeting would be embarrassing to both.

" 'You are right,' said the queen. 'We must not be surprised together. Adieu, then. Tomorrow at the Coliseum;' and we separated."

Madame Récamier, the bosom-friend of Chateaubriand, was in entire political sympathy with the illustrious poet. She regarded legitimacy as a part of her religion, and was intensely devoted to the interests of the Bourbons. She was one of the most beautiful and fascinating women who ever lived. Napoleon at St. Helena, in allusion to this remarkable lady, said:

"I was scarcely First Consul ere I found myself at issue with Madame Récamier. Her father had been placed in the Post-office Department. I had found it necessary to sign, in confidence, a great number of appointments; but I soon established a very rigid inspection in every department. A correspondence was discovered with the Chouans, going on under the connivance of M. Bernard, the father of Madame Récamier. He was immediately dismissed, and narrowly escaped trial and condemnation to death. His daughter hastened to me, and upon her solicitation I exempted M. Bernard from taking his trial, but was resolute respecting his dismissal. Madame Récamier, accustomed to obtain everything, would be satisfied with nothing less than the reinstatement of her father. Such were the morals of the times. My severity excited loud animadversions. It was a thing quite unusual. Madame Récamier and her party never forgave me."[1]

The home of Madame De Staël, who was the very intimate friend of Madame Récamier, became, in the early stages of the Empire, the rendezvous of all those who were intriguing for the overthrow of the government of Napoleon. The Emperor, speaking upon this subject at St. Helena, said:

"The house of Madame De Staël had become quite an arsenal against me. People went there to be armed knights. She endeavored

---

[1] Abbott's *Napoleon at St. Helena*, p. 94.

to raise enemies against me, and fought against me herself. She was at once Armida and Clorinda. It cannot be denied that Madame de Staël is a very distinguished woman. She will go down to posterity. At the time of the Concordat, against which Madame de Staël was violently inflamed, she united at once against me the aristocrats and the republicans. Having at length tired out my patience, she was sent into exile. I informed her that I left her the universe for the theater of her achievements; that I reserved only Paris for myself, which I forbade her to approach, and resigned the rest of the world to her."

The banishment of Madame de Staël from Paris excited as much bitterness in the soul of Madame Récamier as it was possible for a lady of such rare amiability and loveliness of character to feel. Madame Récamier, in giving an account of this transaction, says:

"I had a passionate admiration for Madame de Staël; and this harsh and arbitrary act showed me despotism under its most odious aspect. The man who banished a woman, and such a woman,—who caused her such unhappiness, could only be regarded by me as an unmerciful tyrant; and from that hour I was against him."

The result was that Madame Récamier was forbidden to reside within one hundred and twenty miles of Paris. The reason which Napoleon assigned for these measures was, that Madame de Staël, with the most extraordinary endowments of mind, and Madame Récamier, with charms of personal loveliness which had made her renowned through all Europe, were combining their attractions in forming a conspiracy which would surely deluge the streets of Paris in blood. Napoleon affirmed that though the Government was so strong that it could certainly crush an insurrection in the streets, he thought it better to prohibit these two ladies any further residence in Paris, rather than leave them to foment rebellion, which would cost the lives of many thousands of comparatively innocent persons.

When the Bourbons, at the first restoration, returned to Paris, in the rear of the batteries of the Allies, Madame Récamier again took up her residence in Paris. Her saloons were thronged with the partisans of the old regime, and she was universally recognized as the queen of fashion and beauty. She was in the enjoyment of a very large income, kept her carriage, had a box at the opera, and on opera nights had receptions after the performances. The wheel of fortune had turned, and she was now in the ascendant. Lord Wellington was among her admirers. But the brusque, unpolished duke disgusted the refined French lady by his boast to her, "I have given Napoleon a good beating."

Still the wheel continued its revolution. Napoleon returned from Elba. The Bourbons and their partisans fled precipitately from France. But, in the interim, Madame Récamier and Madame de Staël had dined with the Duchess of St. Leu, at her estate a few leagues from Paris. The return of Napoleon plunged Madame Récamier and her friend into the utmost consternation. She was very unwilling again to leave Paris. In this emergency, Hortense, who was then at the Tuileries, wrote to her under date of March 23, 1815:

> "I hope that you are tranquil. You may trust to me to take care of your interests. I am convinced that I shall not have occasion to show you how delighted I should be to be useful to you. Such would be my desire. But under any circumstances count upon me, and believe that I shall be very happy to prove my friendship for you.
> "Hortense."

The "Hundred Days" passed away. The Bourbons were re-enthroned. Madame Récamier was again a power in Paris. Hortense, deprived of the duchy of St. Leu, was driven an exile out of France. Fifteen years had rolled away, and these two distinguished ladies had not met until the accidental interview to which we have alluded beneath the dome of St. Peter's Cathedral. They were friends, though one was the representative of aristocracy and the other of the rights of the people.

According to the arrangement which they had made, Hortense and Madame Récamier met the next day at the Coliseum. Though it is not to be supposed that Madame Récamier would make any false representations, it is evident that, under the circumstances, she would not soften any of the expressions of Hortense, or represent the conversation which ensued in any light too favorable to Napoleon. We give the narrative, however, of this very interesting interview in the words of Madame Récamier:

"The next day, at the Ave Maria, I was at the Coliseum, where I saw the queen's carriage, which had arrived a few minutes before me. We entered the amphitheater together, complimenting each other on our punctuality, and strolled through this immense ruin as the sun was setting, and to the sound of distant bells.

Interview in the Coliseum.

"Finally we seated ourselves on the steps of the cross in the center of the amphitheater, while Charles Napoleon Bonaparte and M. Ampère, who had followed us, walked about at a little distance. The night came on—an Italian night. The moon rose slowly in the heavens, behind the open arcades of the Coliseum. The breeze of evening sighed through the deserted galleries. Near me sat this woman, herself the living ruin of so extraordinary a fortune. A confused and undefinable emotion forced me to silence. The queen also seemed absorbed in her reflections.

" 'How many events have contributed to bring us together,' she said finally, turning towards me, 'events of which I often have been the puppet or the victim, without having foreseen or provoked them.'

"I could not help thinking that this pretension to the role of a victim was a little hazardous. At that time I was under the conviction that she had not been a stranger to the return from the island of Elba. Doubtless the queen divined my thoughts, since it is hardly possible for me to hide my sentiments. My bearing and face betray me in spite of myself.

" 'I see plainly,' she said earnestly, 'that you share an opinion that has injured me deeply; and it was to controvert it that I wanted to speak to you freely. Henceforth you will justify me, I hope; for I can clear myself of the charge of ingratitude and treason, which would abase me in my own eyes if I had been guilty of them.'

"She was silent a moment and then resumed. 'In 1814, after the abdication of Fontainebleau, I considered that the Emperor had renounced all his rights to the throne, and that his family ought to follow his example. It was my wish to remain in France, under a title that would not give umbrage to the new Government. At the request of the Emperor of Russia, Louis XVIII gave me authority to assume the title of Duchess of St. Leu, and confirmed me in the possession of my private property. In an audience that I obtained to thank him, he treated me with so much courtesy and kindness that I was sincerely grateful; and after having freely accepted his favors I could not think of conspiring against him.

" 'I heard of the landing of the Emperor only through public channels, and it gave me much more annoyance than pleasure. I knew the Emperor too well to imagine that he would have attempted such an enterprise without having certain reasons to hope for success. But the prospect of a civil war afflicted me deeply, and I was convinced

Hortense

that we could not escape it. The speedy arrival of the Emperor baffled all my previsions.

" 'On hearing of the departure of the king, and picturing him to myself old, infirm, and forced to abandon his country again, I was sensibly touched. The idea that he might be accusing me of ingratitude and treason was insupportable to me; and, notwithstanding all the risk of such a step, I wrote to him to exculpate myself from any participation in the events which had just taken place.

" 'On the evening of the 20th of March, being advised of the Emperor's approach by his old minister, I presented myself at the Tuileries to await his coming. I saw him arrive, surrounded, pressed, and borne onward by a crowd of officers of all ranks. In all this tumult I could scarcely accost him. He received me coldly, said a few words to me, and appointed an interview for next day. The Emperor has always inspired me with fear, and his tone on this occasion was not calculated to reassure me. I presented myself, however, with as calm a bearing as was possible. I was introduced into his private room; and we were scarcely alone when he advanced toward me quickly, and said brusquely,

" ' "Have you then so poorly comprehended your situation that you could renounce your name, and the rank you held from me, to accept a title given by the Bourbons?"

" ' "My duty sire," I replied, summoning up all my courage to answer him, "was to think of my children's future, since the abdication of your Majesty left me no longer any other to fulfill."

" ' "Your children," exclaimed the Emperor, "your children! Were they not my nephews before they were your sons? Have you forgotten that? Had you the right to strip them of the rank that belonged to them?" And as I looked at him, all amazed, he added, with increasing rage, "Have you not read the Code, then?"

" 'I avowed my ignorance, recalling to myself that he had formerly considered it reprehensible, in any woman, and especially in members of his own family, to dare to avow that they knew anything about legislation. Then he explained to me with volubility the article in the law prohibiting any change in the state of minors, or the making of any renunciation in their name. As he talked he strode up and down the room, the windows of which were open to admit the beautiful spring sun. I followed him, trying to make him understand that, not knowing the laws, I had only thought of the interests of my children, and taken counsel of my heart. The Emperor stopped all of a sudden, and turning roughly towards me, said,

" ' "Then it should have told you, Madame, that when you shared the prosperity of a family, you ought to know how to submit to its misfortunes."

" 'At these last words I burst into tears. But at this moment our conversation was interrupted by a tremendous uproar which frightened me. The Emperor, while talking, had unconsciously approached the window looking upon the terrace of the Tuileries, which was filled with people, who, upon recognizing him, rent the air with frantic acclamations. The Emperor, accustomed to control himself, saluted the people electrified by his presence, and I hastened to dry my eyes. But they had seen my tears, without the slightest suspicion of their cause. For the next day the papers vied with each other in repeating that the Emperor had shown himself at the windows of the Tuileries, accompanied by Queen Hortense, and that the Queen was so moved by the enthusiasm manifested at the sight of her that she could scarcely restrain her tears.'

"This account," adds Madame Récamier, "had an air of sincerity about it, which shook my previous convictions, and the regard I felt for the Queen was heightened. From that time we became firm friends. We met each other every day, sometimes at the Temple of Vesta, sometimes at the Baths of Titus, or at the Tomb of Cecilia Metella; at others, in some one of the numerous churches of the Christian city, in the rich galleries of its palaces, or at one of the beautiful villas in its environs; and such was our punctuality, that our two carriages almost always arrived together at the appointed place.

"I found the queen a very fascinating companion. And she showed such a delicate tact in respecting the opinions she knew I held, that I could not prevent myself saying that I could only accuse her of the one fault of not being enough of a Bonapartist. Notwithstanding the species of intimacy established between us, I had always abstained from visiting her, when news arrived of the death of Eugene Beauharnais. The Queen loved her brother tenderly. I understood the grief she must feel in losing her nearest relation and the best friend she had in the world, and came quickly to a decision. I immediately went to her, and found her in the deepest affliction. The whole Bonaparte family was there, but that gave me little uneasiness. In such cases it is impossible for me to consider party interests or public opinion. I have been often blamed for this, and probably shall be again, and I must resign myself to this censure, since I shall never cease to deserve it."

Hortense, immediately upon receiving the tidings of the dangerous sickness of her brother, had written thus to Madame Récamier. The letter was dated,

"Rome, Friday morning, April, 1824.

"My Dear Madame,—It seems to be my fate not to be able to enjoy any pleasures, diversions, or interest without the alloy of pain. I have news of my brother. He has been ill. They kindly assure me that he was better when the letter was sent, but I cannot help being extremely anxious. I have a presentiment that this is his last illness, and I am far from him. I trust that God will not deprive me of the only friend left me—the best and most honorable man on earth. I am going to St. Peter's to pray. That will comfort me perhaps, for my very anxiety frightens me. One becomes weak and superstitious in grief. I cannot therefore go with you today, but I shall be happy to see you, if you would like to join me at St. Peter's. I know that you are not afraid of the unhappy, and that you bring them happiness. To wish for you now is enough to prove to you my regard for you.

"Hortense."

Soon after the death of Prince Eugene, Hortense returned to Arenemberg. From that place she wrote to Madame Récamier, under date of June 10th, 1824:

"You were kind enough, Madame, to wish to hear from me. I cannot say that I am well, when I have lost everything on this earth. Meanwhile I am not in ill health. I have just had another heartbreak. I have seen all my brother's things. I do not recoil from this pain, and perhaps I may find in it some consolation. This life, so full of troubles, can disturb no longer the friends for whom we mourn. He, no doubt, is happy. With your sympathies you can imagine all my feelings.

"I am at present in my retreat. The scenery is superb. In spite of the lovely sky of Italy, I still find Arenemberg very beautiful. But I must always be pursued by regrets. It is undoubtedly my fate. Last year I was so contented. I was very proud of not repining, not wishing for anything in this world. I had a good brother, good children. Today how much need have I to repeat to myself that there are still some left to whom I am necessary!

"But I am talking a great deal about myself, and I have nothing to tell you, if it be not that you have been a great comfort to me, and that I shall always be pleased to see you again. You are among those persons to whom it is not needful to relate one's life or one's feelings. The heart is the best interpreter, and they who thus read us become necessary to us.

"I do not ask you about your plans, and nevertheless I am interested to know them. Do not be like me, who live without a future, and who expect to remain where fate puts me; for I may stay at my country-place all winter, if I can have all the rooms heated. Sometimes the wind seems to carry the house off, and the snow, I am told, is of frightful depth. But it requires little courage to surmount these obstacles. On the contrary, these great effects of nature are sometimes not without their charms. Adieu. Do not entirely forget me. Believe me, your friendship has done me good. You know what a comfort a friendly voice from one's native country is, when it comes to us in misfortune and isolation. Be kind enough to tell me that I am unjust if I complain too much of my destiny, and that I have still some friends left.

"Hortense."

Just about this time M. de Chateaubriand, the illustrious friend of Madame Récamier, was quite insultingly dismissed from the ministry for not advocating a law of which the king approved. The disgrace of the minister created a very deep sensation. In allusion to it, Hortense wrote to Madame Récamier, from Arenemberg, Sept. 11, 1824, as follows:

"I expected to hear from you on your return from Naples, and as I have not heard, I know not where to find you. I have fancied that you were on the road to Paris, because I always imagine that we go where the heart goes, and where we can be useful to our friends. It is curious to think what a chain the affections are. Why, I myself, secluded from the world, stranger to everything, am sorry to see so distinguished a man shut out from public life. Is it on account of the interest you have made me take in that quarter, or is it, rather, because, like a Frenchwoman, I love to see merit and superiority honored in my country?

"At present I am no longer alone. I have my cousin with me, the Grand Duchess of Baden, a most accomplished person. The brilliancy of her imagination, the vivacity of her wit, the correctness of her judgment, together with the perfect balance of all her faculties, render her a charming and a remarkable woman. She enlivens my solitude and softens my profound grief. We converse in the language of our country. It is that of the heart, you know, since at Rome we understood each other so well.

"I claim your promise to stop on the way at Arenemberg. It will always be to me very sweet to see you. I cannot separate you from one of my greatest sorrows; which is to say that you are very dear to me, and that I shall be happy to have an opportunity to assure you of my affection.

"HORTENSE."

Madame Récamier, after leaving Rome, kept up her friendly relations and correspondence with Queen Hortense.

The winter of 1829 Hortense spent with her sons in Rome. Chateaubriand was then French ambassador in that city. Upon his leaving, to return to Paris, Hortense wrote to Madame Récamier the following letter, in which she alludes to his departure:

"Rome, May 10, 1829.

"DEAR MADAME,—I am not willing that one of your friends should leave the place where I am living, and where I have had the pleasure of meeting you, without carrying to you a token of my remembrance. I also wish you to convey to him my sentiments. Kindnesses show themselves in the smallest things, and are also felt by those who are the object of them, without their being equal to the expression of their feelings. But the benevolence which has been able to reach me has made me regret not being permitted to know him whom I have learned to appreciate, and who, in a foreign land, so worthily represented to me my country, at least such as I always should like to look upon her, as a friend and protectress.

"I am soon to return to my mountains, where I hope to hear from you. Do not forget me entirely. Remember that I love you, and that your friendship contributed to soothe one of the keenest sorrows of my life. These are two inseparable memories. Thus never doubt my tender love, in again assuring you of which I take such pleasure.

"Hortense."

The year 1830 came. Louis Napoleon was then twenty-two years of age. An insurrection in Paris overthrew the old Bourbon dynasty, and established its modification in the throne of Louis Philippe. This revolution in France threw all Europe into commotion. All over Italy the people rose to cast off the yoke which the Allies, who had triumphed at Waterloo, had imposed upon them. The exiled members of the Bonaparte family met at Rome to decide what to do in the emergency. Hortense attended the meeting with her two sons. The eldest, Napoleon Louis, had married his cousin, the daughter of Joseph Bonaparte. Both of the young princes, with great enthusiasm, joined the patriots. Hortense was very much alarmed for the safety of her sons. She could see but little hope that the insurrection could be successful in Italy, for the "Holy Alliance" was pledged to crush it. She wrote imploringly to her children. Louis Napoleon replied,

"Your affectionate heart will understand our determination. We have contracted engagements which we cannot break. Can we remain deaf to the voice of the unfortunate who call to us? We bear a name which obliges us to listen."

We have not here space to describe the conflict. The Italian patriots, overwhelmed by the armies of Austria, were crushed or dispersed. The elder of the sons of Hortense, Napoleon Louis, died from the fatigue and exposure of the campaign, and was buried at Florence. The younger son, Louis Napoleon, enfeebled by sickness, was in the retreat with the vanquished patriots to Ancona, on the shores of the Adriatic. The distracted mother was hastening to her children when she heard of the death of the one, and of the sickness and perilous condition of the other. She found Louis Napoleon at Ancona, in a burning fever. The Austrians were gathering up the vanquished patriots wherever they could be found in their dispersion, and were mercilessly shooting them. Hortense was in an agony of terror. She knew that her son, if captured, would surely be shot. The Austrians were soon in possession of Ancona. They eagerly sought for the young prince, who bore a name which despots have ever feared. A price was set upon his head. The sagacity of the mother rescued the child. She made arrangements for a frail skiff to steal out from the harbor and cross the Adriatic Sea to the shores of Illyria. Deceived by this stratagem, the Austrian police had no doubt that the young prince had escaped. Their vigilance was accordingly relaxed. Hortense then took a carriage for Pisa. Her son, burning with fever and emaciate from grief and fatigue, mounted the box behind in the disguise of a footman. In this manner, exposed every moment to the danger of being arrested by the Austrian police, the anxious mother and her son traversed the whole breadth of Italy. As Louis Napoleon had, with arms in his hands, espoused the cause of the people in their struggle against Austrian despotism, he could expect no mercy, and there was no safety for him anywhere within reach of the Austrian arm.

By a law of the Bourbons, enacted in 1816, which law was reenacted by the Government of Louis Philippe, no member of the Bonaparte family could enter France but under the penalty of death. But Napoleon I, when in power, had been very generous to the House of Orleans. Hortense, also, upon the return of Napoleon from Elba, when the Royalists were flying in terror from the kingdom, had protected and warmly befriended distinguished members of the family. Under these circumstances, distracted by the fear that her only surviving child would be arrested and shot, and knowing not which way to turn for safety, the mother and the son decided, notwithstanding the menace of death suspended over them, to seek a momentary refuge, incognito, in France.

Embarking in a small vessel, still under assumed names, they safely reached Cannes. At this port Napoleon had landed sixteen years ago, in his marvelous return from Elba. The mother and son proceeded immediately to Paris, resolved to cast themselves upon the generosity of Louis Philippe. Louis Napoleon was still very sick, and needed his bed rather than the fatigues of travel. It was the intention of his mother, so soon as the health of her son was sufficiently restored, to continue their journey and cross over to England.

Hortense, in her *Mémoires,* speaking of these hours of adversity's deepest gloom, writes:

"At length I arrived at the barrier of Paris. I experienced a sort of self-love in exhibiting to my son, by its most beautiful entrance, that capital, of which he could probably retain but a feeble recollection. I ordered the postilion to take us through the Boulevards to the Rue de la Paix, and to stop at the first hotel. Chance conducted us to the Hotel D'Hollande. I occupied a small apartment on the third floor, *du premier,* first above the entresol. From my room I could see the Boulevard and the column in the Place Vendôme. I experienced a sort of saddened pleasure, in my isolation, in once more beholding that city which I was about to leave, perhaps forever, without speaking to a person, and without being distracted by the impression which that view made upon me."

Twenty-two years before, Hortense, in this city, had given birth to the child who was now sick and a fugitive. Austria was thirsting for his blood, and the Government of his own native land had laid upon him the ban of exile, and it was at the peril of their lives that either mother or son placed their feet upon the soil of France. And yet the birth of this prince was welcomed by salvos of artillery, and by every enthusiastic demonstration of public rejoicing, from Hamburg to Rome, and from the Pyrenees to the Danube.

Louis Napoleon was still suffering from a burning fever. A few days of repose seemed essential to the preservation of his life. Hortense immediately wrote a letter to King Louis Philippe, informing him of the arrival of herself and son, incognito, in Paris, of the circumstances which had rendered the step necessary, and casting themselves upon his protection. Louis Philippe owed Hortense a deep debt of gratitude. He had joined the Allies in their war against France. He had come back to Paris in the rear of their batteries. By French law he was a traitor doomed to die. When Napoleon returned from Elba he fled from France in terror, again to join the Allies. He was then the Duke of Orleans. The Duchess of Orleans had slipped upon the stairs and broken her leg. She could not be moved. Both Hortense and Napoleon treated her with the greatest kindness. Of several letters which the Duchess of Orleans wrote Hortense, full of expressions of obligation and gratitude, we will quote but one.

The Duchess of Orleans to Queen Hortense.
"April 19, 1815.

"MADAME,—I am truly afflicted that the feeble state of my health deprives me of the opportunity of expressing to your majesty, as I could wish, my gratitude for the interest she has manifested in my situation. I am still suffering much pain, as my limb has not yet healed. But I cannot defer expressing to your majesty, and to his majesty, the Emperor, to whom I beg you to be my interpreter, the gratitude I feel. I am, madame, your majesty's servant,
"LOUISE MARIE ADELAIDE DE BOURBON,
DUCHESS D'ORLEANS."

The Emperor, in response to the solicitations of Hortense, had permitted the Duchess of Orleans to remain in Paris, and also had assured her of a pension of four hundred thousand francs ($80,000). The Duchess of Bourbon, also, aunt of the Duke of Orleans, was permitted to remain in the city. And she, also, that she might be able to maintain the position due to her rank, received from the Emperor a pension of two hundred thousand francs ($40,000). The Duchess of Bourbon had written to Hortense for some great favors, which Hortense obtained for her. In reply to the assurance of Hortense that she would do what she could to aid her, the duchess wrote, under date of April 29th, 1815:

"I am exceedingly grateful for your kindness, and I have full confidence in the desire which you express to aid me. I can hardly believe that the Emperor will refuse a demand which I will venture to say is so just, and particularly when it is presented by you. Believe me, madame, that my gratitude equals the sentiments of which I beg you to receive, in advance, the most sincere attestation."

Under these circumstances Hortense could not doubt that she might venture to appeal to the magnanimity of the king.

Chapter IX
Life at Arenemberg

It must be confessed that the position of Louis Philippe was painful when he received the note from Hortense announcing that she and her son were in Paris. An insurrection in the streets of Paris had overthrown the throne of the Bourbons, and with it the doctrine of legitimacy. Louis Philippe had been placed upon the vacant throne, not by the voice of the French people, but by a small clique in Paris. There was danger that allied Europe would again rouse itself to restore the Bourbons. Louis Philippe could make no appeal to the masses of the people for support, for he was not the king of their choice. Should he do anything indicative of friendship for the Bonapartes, it might exasperate all dynastic Europe; and should the French people learn that an heir of the Empire was in France, their enthusiasm might produce convulsions the end of which no one could foresee.

Thus unstably seated upon his throne, Louis Philippe was in a state of great embarrassment. He felt that he could not consult the impulses of his heart, but that he must listen to the colder dictates of prudence. He therefore did not venture personally to call upon Queen Hortense, but sent Casimir Périer, president of his council, to see her. As Périer entered her apartment, Hortense said to him:

"Sir, I am a mother. My only means of saving my son was to come to France. I know very well that I have transgressed a law. I am well aware of the risks we run. You have a right to cause our arrest. It would be just."

"Just?" responded the minister, "no; legal? yes." The result of some anxious deliberation was that, in consideration of the alarming sickness of the young prince, they were to be permitted, provided they preserved the strictest incognito, to remain in the city one week. The king also granted Hortense a private audience. He himself knew full well the sorrows of exile. He spoke feelingly of the weary years which he and his family had spent in banishment from France.

"I have experienced," said he to Hortense, "all the griefs of exile. And it is not in accordance with my wishes that yours have not yet ceased." Hortense also saw the queen and the king's sister. There were but these four persons who were allowed to know that Hortense was in Paris. And but two of these, the king and his minister, knew that Prince Louis Napoleon was in the city. But just then came the 5th of May. It was the anniversary of the death of the Emperor at St. Helena. As ever, in this anniversary, immense crowds of the Parisian people gathered around the column on the Place Vendôme with their homage to their beloved Emperor, and covering the railing with wreaths of immortelles and other flowers. Had the populace known that from his window an heir of the great Emperor was looking upon them, it would have created a flame of enthusiasm which scarcely any earthly power could have quenched.

The anxiety of the king, in view of the peril, was so great, that Hortense was informed that the public safety required that she should immediately leave France, notwithstanding the continued sickness of her son. The order was imperative. But both the king and the minister offered her money, that she might continue her journey to London. But Hortense did not need pecuniary aid. She had just cashed at the bank an order for sixteen thousand francs. Before leaving the city, Louis Napoleon wrote to the king a very eloquent and dignified letter, in which he claimed his right, as a French citizen, who had never committed any crime, of residing in his native land. He recognized the king as the representative of a great nation, and earnestly offered his services in defense of his country in the ranks of the army. He avowed that in Italy he had espoused the cause of the people in opposition to aristocratic usurpation, and he demanded the privilege of taking his position, as a French citizen, beneath the tricolor of France.

No reply was returned to this letter. It is said that the spirit and energy it displayed magnified the alarm of the king, and increased his urgency to remove the writer, as speedily as possible, from the soil of France.

On the 6th of May Hortense and her son left Paris, and proceeded that day to Chantilly. Traveling slowly, they were four days in reaching Calais, where they embarked for England. Upon their arrival in London, both Hortense and her son met with a very flattering reception from gentlemen of all parties. For some time they were the guests of the Duke of Bedford, at Woburn Abbey. Talleyrand, who was then French ambassador at the Court of St. James, with characteristic diplomatic caution called himself, and by means of an agent sought to ascertain what were the secret plans and purposes of Queen Hortense.

Several months were passed very profitably in England, and as pleasantly as was possible for persons who had been so long buffeted by the storms of adversity, who were exiles from their native land, and who knew not in what direction to look for a home of safety. While in this state of perplexity, both mother and son were exceedingly gratified by receiving from the Canton of Thurgovia the following document, conferring the rights of citizenship upon the young prince. The document bore the date of Thurgovia, April 30th, 1832.

> "We, the President of the Council of the Canton of Thurgovia, declare that, the Commune of Sallenstein having offered the right of communal citizenship to his highness, Prince Louis Napoleon, out of gratitude for the numerous favors conferred upon the canton by the family of the Duchess of St. Leu, since her residence in Arenemberg; and the grand council having afterwards, by its unanimous vote of the 14th of April, sanctioned this award, and decreed unanimously to his highness the right of honorary burghership of the canton, with the desire of proving how highly it honors the generous character of this family, and how highly it appreciates the preference they have shown for the canton; declares that his highness, Prince Louis Napoleon, son of the Duke and Duchess of St. Leu, is acknowledged as a citizen of the Canton of Thurgovia."

The prince, in the response which he made in the name of his mother and himself, expressed their gratitude for the kindness with which they had ever been treated, and thanked them especially for the honor which they had conferred upon him, in making him the "citizen of a free nation." As a testimonial of his esteem he sent to the authorities of the canton two brass six-pounder cannon, with complete trains and equipage. He also founded a free school in the village of Sallenstein.

Encouraged by these expressions of kindly feeling, both Hortense and her son were very desirous to return to their quiet and much-loved retreat at Arenemberg. The prince, however, who never allowed himself to waste a moment of time, devoted himself, during this short visit to England, assiduously to the study of the workings of British institutions, and to the progress which the nation had attained in the sciences and the arts. It was not easy for Hortense and her son to return to Arenemberg. The Government of Louis Philippe would not permit them to pass through France. Austria vigilantly and indignantly watched every pathway through Italy. They made application for permission to pass through Belgium, but this was denied them. The Belgian throne, which was afterwards offered to Leopold, was then vacant. It was feared that the people would rally at the magic name of Napoleon, and insist that the crown should be placed upon the brow of the young prince.

In this sore dilemma, Louis Philippe at last consented, very reluctantly, that they might pass hurriedly through France, Hortense assuming the name of the Baroness of Arenemberg, and both giving their pledge not to enter Paris. Having obtained the necessary passports, Hortense, with her son, left London in August, and, crossing the Channel, landed at Calais, thus placing their feet once more upon the soil of their native land, from which they were exiled by Bourbon power simply because they bore the name of Bonaparte, which all France so greatly revered. In conformity with their agreement they avoided Paris, though they visited the tomb of Josephine, at Ruel.

They had scarcely reached Switzerland when a deputation of distinguished Poles called upon the young prince, urging him to place himself at the head of their nation, then in arms, endeavoring to regain independence. The letter containing this offer was dated August 31, 1831. It was signed by General Kniazewiez, Count Plater, and many other of the most illustrious men of Poland.

"To whom," it was said, "can the direction of our enterprise be better entrusted than to the nephew of the greatest captain of all ages? A young Bonaparte appearing in our country, tricolor in hand, would produce a moral effect of incalculable consequences. Come, then, young hero, hope of our country. Trust to the waves, which already know your name, the fortunes of Cæsar, and what is more, the destinies of liberty. You will gain the gratitude of your brethren in arms and the admiration of the world."

The chivalric spirit of the young prince was aroused. Notwithstanding the desperation of the enterprise and the great anxiety of his mother, Louis Napoleon left Arenemberg to join the Poles. He had not proceeded far when he received the intelligence that Warsaw was captured and that the patriots were crushed. Sadly he returned to Arenemberg. Again, as ever, he sought solace for his disappointment in intense application to study. In August, 1832, Madame Récamier with M. de Chateaubriand made a visit to Hortense, at the chateau of Arenemberg. The biographer of Madame Récamier in the following terms records this visit:

"In August, 1832, Madame Récamier decided to make a trip to Switzerland, where she was to meet M. de Chateaubriand, who was already wandering in the mountains. She went to Constance. The chateau of Arenemberg, where the Duchess of St. Leu passed her summers, and which she had bought and put in order, overlooks Lake Constance. It was impossible for Madame Récamier not to give a few days to this kind and amiable person, especially in her forlorn and isolated position. The duchess, too, had lost, the year previous, her eldest son, Napoleon, who died in Italy.

"When M. de Chateaubriand joined Madame Récamier at Constance, he was invited to dine with her at the castle. Hortense received him with the most gracious kindness, and read to him some extracts from her own memoirs. The establishment at Arenemberg was elegant, and on a large though not ostentatious scale. Hortense's manners, in her own house, were simple and affectionate. She talked too much, perhaps, about her taste for a life of retirement, love of nature, and aversion to greatness, to be wholly believed. After all these protestations, her visitor could not perceive without surprise the care the duchess and her household took to treat Prince Louis like a sovereign. He had the precedence of everyone.

"The prince, polite, accomplished, and taciturn, appeared to Madame Récamier to be a very different person from his elder brother, whom she had known in Rome, young, generous, and enthusiastic. The prince sketched for her, in sepia, a view of Lake Constance, overlooked by the chateau of Arenemberg. In the foreground a shepherd, leaning against a tree, is watching his flock and playing on the flute. This design, pleasantly associated with Madame Récamier's visit, is now historically interesting. For the last ten years the signature of the author has been affixed to very different things."

But a month before this visit, in July, 1832, Napoleon's only son, the Duke of Reichstadt, died at the age of twenty-one years. All concur in testifying to his noble character. He died sadly, ever cherishing the memory of his illustrious sire, who had passed to the grave through the long agony of St. Helena. The death of the Duke of Reichstadt brought Louis Napoleon one step nearer to the throne of the Empire, according to the vote of the French. There were now but two heirs between him and the crown—his uncle Joseph and his father Louis. Both of these were advanced in life, and the latter exceedingly infirm. The legitimists denied that the people had any right to establish a dynasty; but it was clear that whatever rights popular suffrage could confer would descend to Louis Napoleon upon the death of Joseph and of Louis Bonaparte. Louis Napoleon had no doubt that the immense majority of the French people would improve the first possible opportunity to re-establish the Empire; and consequently the conviction which he so confidently cherished, that he was destined to be the Emperor of France, was not a vague and baseless impression, but the dictate of sound judgment.

The Holy Alliance now contemplated Louis Napoleon with great anxiety, and kept a very close watch upon all his movements. The Government of Louis Philippe was even more unpopular in France than the Government of the elder branch of the Bourbons had been. The crown had not been placed upon his brow either by *legitimacy* or by *popular suffrage,* and there were but few whom he could rally to his support.

With never-flagging zeal the prince prosecuted his studies in the peaceful retreat at Arenemberg, that he might be prepared for the high destiny which he believed awaited him. He published several very important treatises, which attracted the attention of Europe, and which gave him a high position, not merely as a man of letters, but as a statesman of profound views. The *Spectateur Militaire,* in the review of the "Manual of Artillery," by Prince Louis Napoleon, says:

"In looking over this book, it is impossible not to be struck with the laborious industry of which it is the fruit. Of this we can get an idea by the list of authors, French, German, and English, which he has consulted. And this list is no vain catalogue. We can find in the text the ideas, and often the very expressions, of the authorities which he has quoted. When we consider how much study and perseverance must have been employed to succeed in producing only the literary part (for even the illustrations scattered through the work are from the author's own designs) of a book which requires such profound and varied attainments, and when we remember that this author was born on the steps of a throne, we cannot help being seized with admiration for the man who thus bravely meets the shocks of adversity."

A gentleman, in a work entitled *Letters from London,* in the following language describes the prince's mode of life at Arenemberg:

"From his tenderest youth Prince Louis Napoleon has despised the habits of an effeminate life. Although his mother allowed him a considerable sum for his amusements, these were the last things he thought of. All this money was spent in acts of beneficence, in founding schools or houses of refuge, in printing his military or political works, or in making scientific experiments. His mode of life was always frugal, and rather rude. At Arenemberg it was quite military.

"His room, situated not in the castle, but in a small pavilion beside it, offered none of the grandeur or elegance so prevalent in Hortense's apartment. It was, in truth, a regular soldier's tent. Neither carpet nor armchair appeared there; nothing that could indulge the body; nothing but books of science and arms of all kinds. As for himself, he was on horseback at break of day, and before anyone had risen in the castle he had ridden several leagues. He then went to work in his cabinet. Accustomed to military exercises, as good a rider as could be seen, he never let a day pass without devoting some hours to sword and lance practice and the use of infantry arms, which he managed with extraordinary rapidity and address."

His personal appearance at that time is thus graphically sketched. "He is middle-sized, of an agreeable countenance, and has a military air. To personal advantages he joins the more seductive distinction of manners simple, natural, and full of good taste and ease. At first sight I was struck with his resemblance to Prince Eugene, and to the Empress Josephine, his grandmother. But I did not remark a like resemblance to the Emperor. But by attentively observing the essential features, that is those not depending on more or less fullness or on more or less beard, we soon discover that the Napoleonic type is reproduced with astonishing fidelity. It is, in fact, the same lofty forehead, broad and straight, the same nose, of fine proportions, the same gray eyes, though, the expression is milder. It is particularly the same contour and inclination of the head. The latter especially, when the prince turns, is so full of the Napoleon air, as to make a soldier of the Old Guard thrill at the sight. And if the eye rests on the outline

The study of Louis Napoleon.

of these forms, it is impossible not to be struck, as if before the head of the Emperor, with the imposing grandeur of the Roman profile, of which the lines, so defined, so grave, I will even add and so solemn, are, as it were, the soul of great destinies.

"The distinguishing expression of the features of the young prince is that of nobleness and gravity. And yet, far from being harsh, his countenance, on the contrary, breathes a sentiment of mildness and benevolence. It seems that the maternal type which is preserved in the lower part of his face has come to correct the rigidity of the imperial lines, as the blood of the Beauharnais seems to have tempered in him the southern violence of the Napoleon blood. But what excites the greatest interest is that indefinable tinge of melancholy and thoughtfulness observable in the slightest movement, and revealing the noble sufferings of exile.

"But after this portrait you must not figure to yourself one of those elegant young men, those Adonises of romance who excite the admiration of the drawing room. There is nothing of effeminacy in the young Napoleon. The dark shadows of his countenance indicate an energetic nature. His assured look, his glance at once quick and thoughtful, everything about him points out one of those exceptional natures, one of those great souls that live by meditating on great things, and that alone are capable of accomplishing them."

About this time the young prince wrote as follows to his friend, the poet Belmontet: "Still far from my country, and deprived of all that can render life dear to a manly heart, I yet endeavor to retain my courage in spite of fate, and find my only consolation in hard study. Adieu. Sometimes think of all the bitter thoughts which must fill my mind when I contrast the past glories of France with her present condition and hopeless future. It needs no little courage to press on alone, as one can, towards the goal which one's heart has vowed to reach. Nevertheless I must not despair, the honor of France has so many elements of vitality in it."

Some months later he wrote to the same friend: "My life has been until now marked only by profound griefs and stifled wishes. The blood of Napoleon rebels in my veins, in not being able to flow for the national glory. Until the present time there has been nothing remarkable in my life, excepting my birth. The sun of glory shone upon my cradle. Alas! that is all. But who can complain when the Emperor has suffered so much? Faith in the future, such is my only hope; the sword of the Emperor my only stay; a glorious death for France my ambition. Adieu! Think of the poor exiles, whose eyes are ever turned towards the beloved shores of France. And believe that my heart will never cease to beat at the sound of country, honor, patriotism, and devotion."

Hortense deeply sympathized in the sorrows of her son. Like the caged eagle, he was struggling against his bars, longing for a lofty flight. On the 10th of August, 1834, she wrote to their mutual friend, Belmontet as follows:

> "The state of my affairs obliges me to remain during the winter in my mountain home, exposed to all its winds. But what is this compared with the dreadful sufferings which the Emperor endured upon the rock of St. Helena? I would not complain if my son, at his age, did not find himself deprived of all society and completely isolated, without any diversion but the laborious pursuits to which he is devoted. His courage and strength of soul equal his sad and painful destiny. What a generous nature! What a good and noble young man! I am proud to be his mother, and I should admire him if I were not so. I rejoice as much in the nobleness of his character, as I grieve at being unable to render his life more happy. He was born for better things. He is worthy of them. We contemplate passing a couple of months at Geneva. There he will at least hear the French language spoken. That will be an agreeable change for him. The mother tongue, is it not almost one's country?"

It every day became more and more evident that the throne of Louis Philippe, founded only upon the stratagem of a clique in Paris, could not stand long. Under these circumstances, one of the leading Republicans in Paris wrote to the prince as follows:

> "The life of the king is daily threatened. If one of these attempts should succeed, we should be exposed to the most serious convulsions; for there is no longer in France any party which can lead the others, nor any man who can inspire general confidence. In this position, prince, we have turned our eyes to you. The great name which you bear, your opinions, your character, everything induces us to see in you

a point of rallying for the popular cause. Hold yourself ready for action, and when the time shall come your friends will not fail you."

The Government of Louis Philippe had been constrained by the demand of the French people to restore to the summit of the column in the Place Vendôme the statue of Napoleon, which the Allies had torn from it. As the colossal image of the Emperor was raised to its proud elevation on that majestic shaft, the utmost enthusiasm pervaded not only the streets of the metropolis, but entire France. Day after day immense crowds gathered in the place, garlanding the railing with wreaths of immortelles, and exhibiting enthusiasm which greatly alarmed the Government.

Hortense and Louis, from their place of exile, watched these popular demonstrations with intensest interest. All France seemed to be honoring Napoleon. And yet neither Hortense nor her son were allowed by the Government to touch the soil of France under penalty of death, simply because they were relatives of Napoleon. The completion of the Arc de l'Etoile, at the head of the avenue of the Champs Elysee, a work which Napoleon had originated, was another reminder to the Parisians of the genius of the great Emperor.

The Emperor, with dying breath, had said at St. Helena, "It is my wish that my ashes may repose on the banks of the Seine, in the midst of the French people whom I have loved so well." All France was now demanding that this wish should be fulfilled. The Government dared not attempt to resist the popular sentiment. The remains were demanded of England, and two frigates were sent to transport them to France. And the whole kingdom prepared to receive those remains, and honor them with a burial more imposing than had ever been conferred upon a mortal before.

Louis Napoleon and his friends thought that the time had now arrived in which it was expedient for him to present himself before the people of France, and claim their protection from the oppression of the French Government. It was believed that the French people, should the opportunity be presented them, would rise at the magic name of Napoleon, overthrow the throne of Louis Philippe, and then, by the voice of universal suffrage, would re-establish the Empire.

This would place Joseph Bonaparte on the throne, and would at once annul the decree of banishment against the whole Bonaparte family. Hortense and Louis Napoleon could then return to their native land. As Louis Napoleon was in the direct line of hereditary descent, the re-establishment of the Empire would undoubtedly in the end secure the crown for Louis Napoleon. The ever-increasing enthusiasm manifested for the memory of Napoleon I, and the almost universal unpopularity of the Government of Louis Philippe, led Louis Napoleon and his friends to think that the time had come for the restoration of the Empire, or rather to restore to the people the right of universal suffrage, that they might choose a republic or empire or a monarchy, as the people should judge best for the interests of France.

It so happened that there was, at that time, in garrison at Strasburg the same regiment in which General Bonaparte so brilliantly commenced his career at the siege of Toulon, and which had received him with so much enthusiasm at Grenoble, on his return from Elba, and had escorted him in his triumphant march to Paris. Colonel Vaudrey, a very enthusiastic and eloquent young man who had great influence over his troops, was in command of the regiment. It was not doubted that these troops would with enthusiasm rally around an heir of the Empire. In preparation for the movement, Louis Napoleon held several interviews with Colonel Vaudrey at Baden. In one of these interviews the prince said to the colonel:

"The days of prejudice are past. The prestige of divine right has vanished from France with the old institutions. A new era has commenced. Henceforth the people are called to the free development of their faculties. But in this general impulse, impressed by modern civilization, what can regulate the movement? What government will be sufficiently strong to assure to the country the enjoyment of public liberty without agitations, without disorders? It is necessary for a free people that they should have a government of immense moral force. And this moral force, where can it be found, if not in the right and the will of all? So long as a general vote has not sanctioned a government, no matter what that government may be, it is not built upon a solid foundation. Adverse factions will constantly agitate society; while institutions ratified by the voice of the nation will lead to the abolition of parties and will annihilate individual resistances.

"A revolution is neither legitimate nor excusable except when it is made in the interests of the majority of the nation. One may be sure that this is the motive which influences him, when he makes use of moral influences only to attain his ends. If the Government have committed so many faults as to render a revolution desirable for the nation, if the Napoleonic cause have left sufficiently deep remembrances in French hearts, it will be enough, for me merely to present myself before the soldiers and the people, recalling to their memory their recent griefs and past glory, for them to flock around my standard.

"If I succeed in winning over a regiment, if the soldiers to whom I am unknown are roused by the sight of the imperial eagle, then all the chances will be mine. My cause will be morally gained, even if secondary obstacles rise to prevent its success. It is my aim to present a popular flag—the most popular, the most glorious of all,—which shall serve as a rallying-point for the generous and the patriotic of all parties; to restore to France her dignity without universal war, her liberty without license, her stability without despotism. To arrive at such a result, what must be done? One must receive from the people alone all his power and all his rights."

The man who should undertake in this way to overthrow an established government, must of course peril his life. If unsuccessful, he could anticipate no mercy. Hortense perceived with anxiety that the mind of her son was intensely absorbed in thoughts which he did not reveal to her. On the morning of the 25th of October, 1836, Louis Napoleon bade adieu to his mother, and left Arenemberg in his private carriage, ostensibly to visit friends at Baden. A few days after, Hortense was plunged into the deepest distress by the reception of the following letter:

> "MY DEAR MOTHER,—You must have been very anxious in receiving no tidings from me—you who believed me to be with my cousin. But your inquietude will be redoubled when you learn that I made an attempt at Strasburg, which has failed. I am in prison, with several other officers. It is for them only that I suffer. As for myself, in commencing such an enterprise, I was prepared for everything. Do not weep, mother. I am the victim of a noble cause, of a cause entirely French. Hereafter justice will be rendered me and I shall be commiserated.
>
> "Yesterday morning I presented myself before the Fourth Artillery, and was received with cries of *Vive l'Empereur!* For a time all went well. The Forty-sixth resisted. We were captured in the courtyard of their barracks. Happily no French blood was shed. This consoles me in my calamity. Courage, my

mother! I shall know how to support, even to the end, the honor of the name I bear. Adieu! Do not uselessly mourn my lot. Life is but a little thing. Honor and France are everything to me. I embrace you with my whole heart. Your tender and respectful son,

"Louis Napoleon Bonaparte.
"Strasburg, November 1, 1836."

Hortense immediately hastened to France, to do whatever a mother's love and anguish could accomplish for the release of her son, though in crossing the frontiers she knew that she exposed herself to the penalty of death. Apprehensive lest her presence in Paris might irritate the Government, she stopped at Viry, at the house of the Duchess de Raguse. Madame Récamier repaired at once to Viry to see Hortense, where she found her in great agony. Soon, however, a mother's fears were partially relieved, as the Government of Louis Philippe, knowing the universal enthusiasm with which the Emperor and the Empire were regarded, did not dare to bring the young prince to trial, or even to allow it to be known that he was upon the soil of France. With the utmost precipitation they secretly hurried their prisoner through France, by day and by night, to the seaboard, where he was placed on board a frigate, whose captain had sealed instructions respecting the destination of his voyage, which he was not to open until he had been several days at sea.

Poor Hortense, utterly desolate and heartbroken, returned to Arenemberg. She knew that the life of her son had been spared, and that he was to be transported to some distant land. But she knew not where he would be sent, or what would be his destiny there. It is however probable that ere long she learned, through her numerous friends, what were the designs of the Government respecting him. She however never saw her son again until, upon a dying bed, she gave him her last embrace and blessing. The hurried journey, and the terrible anxiety caused by the arrest and peril of her son, inflicted a blow upon Hortense from which she never recovered. Weary months passed away in the solitude of Arenemberg, until at last the heart-stricken mother received a package of letters from the exile. As the narrative contained in these letters throws very interesting light upon the character of the mother as well as of the son, we shall insert it in the next chapter.

Chapter X
Letter from Louis Napoleon to His Mother

"My Mother,—To give you a detailed recital of my misfortunes is to renew your griefs and mine. And still it is a consolation, both for you and for me, that you should be informed of all the impressions which I have experienced, and of all the emotions which have agitated me since the end of October. You know what was the pretext which I gave when I left Arenemberg. But you do not know what was then passing in my heart. Strong in my conviction which led me to look upon the Napoleonic cause as the only national cause in France, as the only civilizing cause in Europe, proud of the nobility and purity of my intentions, I was fully resolved to raise the imperial eagle, or to fall the victim of my political faith.

"I left, taking in my carriage the same route which I had followed three months before when going from Urkirch to Baden. Everything was the same around me. But what a difference in the impressions with which I was animated! I was then cheerful and serene as the unclouded day. But now, sad and thoughtful, my spirit had taken the hue of the air, gloomy and chill, which surrounded me. I may be asked, what could have induced me to abandon a happy existence, to encounter all the risks of a hazardous enterprise. I reply that a secret voice constrained me; and that nothing in the world could have induced me to postpone to another period an attempt which seemed to me to present so many chances of success.

"And the most painful thought for me at this moment is—now that reality has come to take the place of suppositions, and that, instead of imagining, I have seen—that I am firm in the belief that if I had followed the plan which I had marked out for myself, instead of being now under the Equator, I

Hortense

should be in my own country. Of what importance to me are those vulgar ones which call me insensate because I have not succeeded, and which would have exaggerated my merit had I triumphed? I take upon myself all the responsibility of the movement, for I have acted from conviction, and not from the influence of others. Alas! if I were the only victim I should have nothing to deplore. I have found in my friends boundless devotion, and I have no reproaches to make against any one whatever.

"On the 27th I arrived at Lahr, a small town of the Grandduchy of Baden, where I awaited intelligence. Near that place the axle of my carriage broke, and I was compelled to remain there for a day. On the morning of the 28th I left Lahr, and, retracing my steps, passed through Fribourg, Neubrisach, and Colmar, and arrived, at eleven o'clock in the evening, at Strasburg without the least embarrassment. My carriage was taken to the *Hotel de la Fleur,* while I went to lodge in a small chamber, which had been engaged for me, in the *Rue de la Fontaine.*

"There I saw, on the 29th, Colonel Vaudrey, and submitted to him the plan of operations which I had drawn up. But the colonel, whose noble and generous sentiments merited a better fate, said to me:

" 'There is no occasion here for a conflict with arms. Your cause is too French and too pure to be soiled in shedding French blood. There is but one mode of procedure which is worthy of you, because it will avoid all collision. When you are at the head of my regiment we will march together to General Voirol's.[1] An old soldier will not resist the sight of you and of the imperial eagle when he knows that the garrison follows you.'

"I approved his reasons, and all things were arranged for the next morning. A house had been engaged in a street in the neighborhood of the quarter of Austerlitz, whence we all were to proceed to those barracks as soon as the regiment of artillery was assembled.

"Upon the 29th, at eleven o'clock in the evening, one of my friends came to seek me at the *Rue de la Fontaine,* to

---
[1] The commanding officer of the garrison.

conduct me to the general rendezvous. We traversed together the whole city. A bright moon illuminated the streets. I regarded the fine weather as a favorable omen for the next day. I examined with care the places through which I passed. The silence which reigned made an impression upon me. By what would that calm be replaced tomorrow!

" 'Nevertheless,' said I to my companion, 'there will be no disorder if I succeed. It is especially to avoid the troubles which frequently accompany popular movements that I have wished to make the revolution by means of the army. But,' I added, 'what confidence, what profound conviction must we have of the nobleness of our cause, to encounter not merely the dangers which we are about to meet, but that public opinion which will load us with reproaches and overwhelm us if we do not succeed! And still, I call God to witness that it is not to satisfy a personal ambition, but because I believe that I have a mission to fulfill, that I risk that which is more dear to me than life, the esteem of my fellow-citizens.'

"Having arrived at the house in the *Rue des Orphelins*, I found my friends assembled in two apartments on the ground floor. I thanked them for the devotion which they manifested for my cause, and said to them that from that hour we would share good and bad fortune together. One of the officers had an eagle. It was that which had belonged to the seventh regiment of the line. 'The eagle of Labédoyère,'[1] one exclaimed, and each one of us pressed it to his heart with

---

[1] Colonel Labédoyère was a young man of fine figure and elegant manners, descended from a respectable family, and whose heart ever throbbed warmly in remembrance of the glories of the Empire. Upon the abdication of Napoleon and his retirement to Elba, Labédoyère was in command of the seventh regiment of the line, stationed at Grenoble. He fraternized with his troops in the enthusiasm with which one and all were swept away at the sight of the returning Emperor. Drawing a silver eagle from his pocket, he placed it upon the flagstaff and embraced it in the presence of all his soldiers, who, in a state of the wildest excitement, with shouts of joy, gathered around Napoleon, crying *Vive l'Empereur!*
After Waterloo and the exile to St. Helena, Labédoyère was arrested, tried, and shot. It is said that the judges shed tears when they condemned the noble young man to death. His young wife threw herself at the feet of Louis XVIII, and, frantic with grief, cried out, "Pardon, sire, pardon!" Louis replied, "My duty as a king ties my hands. I can only pray for the soul of him whom justice has condemned."— Abbott's *The Life of Napoleon Bonaparte*, vol. ii. p. 110.

lively emotion. All the officers were in full uniform. I had put on the uniform of the artillery and the hat of a major-general.

"The night seemed to us very long. I spent it in writing my proclamations, which I had not been willing to have printed in advance for fear of some indiscretion. It was decided that we should remain in that house until the colonel should notify me to proceed to the barracks. We counted the hours, the minutes, the seconds. Six o'clock in the morning was the moment indicated.

"How difficult it is to express what one experiences under such circumstances. In a second one lives more than in ten years; for to live is to make use of our organs, our senses, our faculties—of all the parts of ourselves which impart the sentiment of our existence. And in these critical moments our faculties, our organs, our senses, exalted to the highest degree, are concentrated on one single point. It is the hour which is to decide our entire destiny. One is strong when he can say to himself, 'Tomorrow I shall be the liberator of my country, or I shall be dead.' One is greatly to be pitied when circumstances are such that he can neither be one nor the other.

"Notwithstanding my precautions, the noise which a certain number of persons meeting together cannot help making, awoke the occupants of the first story. We heard them rise and open their windows. It was five o'clock. We redoubled our precautions, and they went to sleep again.

"At last the clock struck six. Never before did the sound of a clock vibrate so violently in my heart. But a moment after the bugle from the quarter of Austerlitz came to accelerate its throbbings. The great moment was approaching. A very considerable tumult was heard in the street. Soldiers passed shouting; horsemen rode at full gallop by our windows. I sent an officer to ascertain the cause of the tumult. Had the chief officer of the garrison been informed of our projects? Had we been discovered? My messenger soon returned to say to me that the noise came from some soldiers whom the colonel had sent to fetch their horses, which were outside the quarter.

"A few more minutes passed, and I was informed that the colonel was waiting for me. Full of hope, I hastened into the street. M. Parguin,[1] in the uniform of a brigadier-general, and a commander of battalion, carrying the eagle in his hand, are by my side. About a dozen officers follow me.

"The distance was short; it was soon traversed. The regiment was drawn up in line of battle in the barrack-yard, inside of the rails. Upon the grass forty of the horse-artillery were stationed.

"My mother, judge of the happiness I experienced at that moment. After twenty-years of exile, I touched again the sacred soil of my country. I found myself with Frenchmen whom the recollection of the Empire was again to electrify.

"Colonel Vaudrey was alone in the middle of the yard. I directed my steps towards him. Immediately the colonel, whose noble countenance and fine figure had at that moment something of the sublime, drew his sword and exclaimed:

" 'Soldiers of the Fourth Regiment of Artillery! A great revolution is being accomplished at this moment. You see here before you the nephew of the Emperor Napoleon. He comes to reconquer the rights of the people. The people and the army can rely upon him. It is around him that all should rally who love the glory and the liberty of France. Soldiers! you must feel, as does your chief, all the grandeur of the enterprise you are about to undertake, all the sacredness of the cause you are about to defend. Soldiers! can the nephew of the Emperor rely upon you?'

"His voice was instantly drowned by unanimous cries of *Vive Napoleon! Vive l'Empereur!* I then addressed them in the following words:

" 'Resolved to conquer or to die for the cause of the French people, it is to you first that I wish to present myself, because between you and me exist grand recollections. It is in your regiment that the Emperor, my uncle, served as captain. It is with you that he made his name famous at the siege of Toulon, and it is your brave regiment again which opened to him the gates of Grenoble, on his return from the isle of Elba.

---

[1] M. Parguin was the gentleman to whom we have before alluded, who was a highly esteemed young officer under Napoleon I, and who, having married Mademoiselle Cotelet, the reader of Queen Hortense, had purchased the estate of Wolfberg, in the vicinity of Arenemberg, and became one of the most intimate friends of Prince Louis Napoleon.

Soldiers! new destinies are reserved for you. To you belongs the glory of commencing a great enterprise; to you the honor of first saluting the eagle of Austerlitz and of Wagram.'

"I then seized the eagle-surmounted banner, which one of my officers, M. de Carelles, bore, and presenting it to them, said,

" 'Soldiers! behold the symbol of the glory of France. During fifteen years it conducted our fathers to victory. It has glittered upon all the fields of battle. It has traversed all the capitals of Europe. Soldiers! will you not rally around this noble standard which I confide to your honor and to your courage? Will you not march with me against the traitors and the oppressors of our country to the cry, *Vive la France! Vive la liberté!?*'

"A thousand affirmative cries responded to me. We then commenced our march, music in front. Joy and hope beamed from every countenance. The plan was, to hasten to the house of the general, and to present to him, not a dagger at his throat, but the eagle before his eyes. It was necessary, in order to reach his house, to traverse the whole city. While on the way, I had to send an officer with a guard to publish my proclamations; another to the prefect, to arrest him. In short, six received special missions, so that when I arrived at the general's, I had voluntarily parted with a considerable portion of my forces.

"But had I then necessity to surround myself with so many soldiers? could I not rely upon the participation of the people? and, in fine, whatever may be said, along the whole route which I traversed I received unequivocal signs of the sympathy of the population. I had actually to struggle against the vehemence of the marks of interest which were lavished upon me; and the variety of cries which greeted me showed that there was no party which did not sympathize with my feelings.

"Having arrived at the court of the hotel of the general, I ascended the stairs, followed by Messieurs Vaudrey, Parguin, and two officers. The general was not yet dressed. I said to him,

"'General, I come to you as a friend. I should be sorry to raise our old tricolor banner without the aid of a brave soldier like you. The garrison is in my favor. Decide and follow me.'

"The eagle was presented to him. He rejected it, saying, 'Prince, they have deceived you. The army knows its duties, as I will prove to you immediately.'

"I then departed, and gave orders to leave a file of men to guard him. The general afterwards presented himself to his soldiers, to induce them to return to obedience. The artillerymen, under the orders of M. Parguin, disregarded his authority, and replied to him only by reiterated cries of *Vive l'Empereur*. Subsequently the general succeeded in escaping from his hotel by an unguarded door.

"When I left the hotel of the general, I was greeted with the same acclamations of *Vive l'Empereur*. But this first check had already seriously affected me. I was not prepared for it, convinced as I had been that the sight alone of the eagle would recall to the general the old souvenirs of glory, and would lead him to join us.

"We resumed our march. Leaving the main street, we entered the barracks of Finkematt, by the lane which leads there through the Faubourg of Pierre. This barrack is a large building, erected in a place with no outlet but the entrance. The ground in front is too narrow for a regiment to be drawn up in line of battle. In seeing myself thus hedged in between the ramparts and the barracks, I perceived that the plan agreed upon had not been followed out. Upon our arrival, the soldiers thronged around us. I harangued them. Most of them went to get their arms, and returned to rally around me, testifying their sympathy for me by their acclamations.

"However, seeing them manifest a sudden hesitation, caused by the reports circulated by some officers among them who endeavored to inspire them with doubts of my identity, and as we were also losing precious time in an unfavorable position, instead of hastening to the other regiments who expected us, I requested the colonel to depart. He urged me to remain a little longer. I complied with his advice.

"Some infantry officers arrived, ordered the gates to be closed, and strongly reprimanded their soldiers. The soldiers hesitated. I ordered the arrest of the officers. Their soldiers rescued them. Then all was confusion. The space was so contracted that each one was lost in the crowd. The people, who had climbed upon the wall, threw stones at the infantry. The cannoneers wished to use their arms, but we prevented it. We saw clearly that it would cause the death of very many. I saw the colonel by turns arrested by the infantry, and rescued by his soldiers. I was myself upon the point of being slain by a multitude of men who, recognizing me, crossed their bayonets upon me. I parried their thrusts with my saber, trying at the same time to calm them, when the cannoneers rescued me from their guns, and placed me in the middle of themselves.

"I then pressed forward, with some subaltern officers, towards the mounted artillery men, to seize a horse. All the infantry followed me. I found myself hemmed in between the horses and the wall, without power to move. Then the soldiers, arriving from all parts, seized me and conducted me to the guard-house. On entering I found M. Parguin. I extended my hand to him. He said to me, speaking in tones calm and resigned, 'Prince, we shall be shot, but it will be in a good cause.'

" 'Yes,' I replied, 'we have fallen in a grand and a glorious enterprise.'

"Soon after General Voirol arrived. He said to me, upon entering,

" 'Prince, you have found but one traitor in the French army.'

" 'Say rather, general,' I replied, 'that I have found one Labédoyère.' Some carriages were soon brought, and we were transported to the new prison.

"Behold me, then, between four walls, with barred windows, in the abode of criminals. Ah! those who know what it is to pass in an instant from the excess of happiness, caused by the noblest illusions, to the excess of misery, which leaves no hope, and to pass over this immense interval without having one moment to prepare for it, alone can comprehend what was passing in my heart.

"At the lodge we met again. M. de Querelles, pressing my hand, said to me in a loud voice, 'Prince, notwithstanding our

The arrest.

defeat, I am still proud of what we have done.' They subjected me to an interrogation. I was calm and resigned. My part was taken. The following questions were proposed to me:

" 'What has induced you to act as you have done?'

" 'My political opinions,' I replied, 'and my desire to return to my country, from which a foreign invasion has exiled me. In 1830, I demanded to be treated as a simple citizen. They treated me as a pretender. Well, I have acted as a pretender.'

" 'Did you wish,' it was asked, 'to establish a military government?'

" 'I wished,' was my reply, 'to establish a government based on popular election.'

" 'What would you have done if successful?'

" 'I would have assembled a national Congress.'

"I declared then, that I alone having organized everything, that I alone having induced others to join me, the whole responsibility should fall upon my head alone. Reconducted to prison, I threw myself upon a bed which had been prepared for me, and, notwithstanding my torments, sleep, which soothes suffering, in giving repose to the anguish of the soul, came to calm my senses. Repose does not fly from the couch of the unfortunate. It only avoids those who are consumed by remorse. But how frightful was my awaking. I thought that I had had a dreadful nightmare. The fate of the persons who were compromised caused me the greatest grief and anxiety. I wrote to General Voirol, to say to him that his honor obliged him to interest himself in behalf of Colonel Vaudrey; for it was, perhaps, the attachment of the colonel for him, and the regard with which he had treated him, which were the causes of the failure of my enterprise. I closed in beseeching him that all the rigor of the law might fall upon me, saying that I was the most guilty, and the only one to be feared.

"The general came to see me, and was very affectionate. He said, upon entering, 'Prince, when I was your prisoner, I could find no words sufficiently severe to say to you. Now that you are mine, I have only words of consolation to offer.' Colonel Vaudrey and I were conducted to the citadel, where I, at least, was much more comfortable than in prison. But the civil power claimed us, and at the end of twenty-four hours we were conveyed back to our former abode.

"The jailer and the director of the prison at Strasburg did their duty; but they endeavored to alleviate as much as possible my situation, while a certain M. Lebel, who had been sent from Paris, wishing to show his authority, prevented me from opening my windows to breathe the air, took from me my watch, which he only restored to me at the moment of my departure, and, in fine, even ordered blinds to intercept the light.

"On the evening of the 9th I was told that I was to be transferred to another prison. I went out and met the general and the prefect, who took me away in their carriage without informing me where I was to be conducted. I insisted that I should be left with my companions in misfortune. But the Government had decided otherwise. Upon arriving at the hotel of the prefecture, I found two post-chaises. I was ordered into one with M. Cuynat, commander of the gendarmerie of the Seine, and Lieutenant Thiboutot. In the other there were four sub-officers.

"When I perceived that I was to leave Strasburg, and that it was my lot to be separated from the other accused, I experienced anguish difficult to be described. Behold me, then, forced to abandon the men who had devoted themselves to me. Behold me deprived of the means of making known in my defense my views and my intentions. Behold me receiving a so-called favor from him upon whom I had wished to inflict the greatest evil. I vented my sorrow in complaints and regrets. I could only protest.

"The two officers who conducted me were two officers of the Empire, intimate friends of M. Parguin. Thus they treated me with the kindest attentions. I could have thought myself traveling with friends. Upon the 11th, at two o'clock in the morning, I arrived at Paris, at the hotel of the Prefecture of Police. M. Delessat was very polite to me. He informed me that you had come to France to claim in my favor the clemency of the king, and that I was to start again in two hours for Lorient, and that thence I was to sail for the United States in a French frigate.

"I said to the prefect that I was in despair in not being permitted to share the fate of my companions in misfortune; that being thus withdrawn from prison before undergoing a general examination (the first had been only a summary one), I was deprived of the means of testifying to many facts in favor of the accused. But my protestations were unavailing. I decided to write to the king. And I said to him that, having been cast into prison after having taken up arms against his Government, I dreaded but one thing, and that was his generosity, since it would deprive me of my sweetest consolation, the possibility of sharing the fate of my companions in misfortune. I added that life itself was of little value to me; but that my gratitude to him would be great if he would spare the lives of a few old soldiers, the remains of our ancient army, who had been enticed by me, and seduced by glorious souvenirs.

"At the same time I wrote to M. Odillon Barrot[1] the letter which I send with this, begging him to take charge of the defense of Colonel Vaudrey. At four o'clock I resumed my journey, with the same escort, and on the 14th we arrived at the citadel of Port Louis, near Lorient. I remained there until the twenty-first day of November, when the frigate was ready for sea.

"After having entreated M. Odillon Barrot to assume the defense of the accused, and in particular of Colonel Vaudrey, I added:

" 'Monsieur, notwithstanding my desire to remain with my companions in misfortune, and to partake of their lot, notwithstanding my entreaties upon that subject, the king, in his clemency, has ordered that I should be conducted to Lorient, to pass thence to America. Sensible as I ought to be of the generosity of the king, I am profoundly afflicted in leaving my co-accused, since I cherish the conviction that could I be present at the bar, my depositions in their favor would influence the jury, and enlighten them as to their decision. Deprived of the consolation of being useful to the men whom I have enticed to their loss, I am obliged to entrust to an advocate that which I am unable to say myself to the jury.

---

[1] A distinguished advocate in Paris.

" 'On the part of my co-accused there was no plot. There was only the enticement of the moment. I alone arranged all. I alone made the necessary preparations. I had already seen Colonel Vaudrey before the 30th of October, but he had not conspired with me. On the 29th, at eight o'clock in the evening, no person knew but myself that the movement was to take place the next day. I did not see Colonel Vaudrey until after this. M. Parguin had come to Strasburg on his own private business. It was not until the evening of the 29th, that I appealed to him. The other persons knew of my presence in France, but were ignorant of the object of my visit. It was not until the evening of the 29th that I assembled the persons now accused; and I did not make them acquainted with my intentions until that moment.

" 'Colonel Vaudrey was not present. The officers of the engineers had come to join us, ignorant at first of what was to transpire. Certainly, in the eyes of the established Government we are all culpable of having taken up arms against it. But I am the most culpable. It is I who, for a long time meditating a revolution, came suddenly to lure men from an honorable social position, to expose them to the hazards of a popular movement. Before the laws, my companions are guilty of allowing themselves to be enticed. But never were circumstances more extenuating in the eyes of the country than those in their favor. When I saw Colonel Vaudrey and the other persons on the evening of the 29th, I addressed them in the following language:

" ' "Gentlemen,—You are aware of all the complaints of the nation against the Government. But you also know that there is no party now existing which is sufficiently strong to overthrow it; no one sufficiently strong to unite the French of all parties, even if it should succeed in taking possession of supreme power. This feebleness of the Government, as well as this feebleness of parties, proceeds from the fact that each one represents only the interests of a single class in society. Some rely upon the clergy and nobility; others upon the middle-class aristocracy, and others still upon the lower classes alone.

" ' "In this state of things, there is but a single flag which can rally all parties, because it is the banner of France, and not that of a faction; it is the eagle of the Empire. Under this banner, which recalls so many glorious memories, there is no class excluded. It represents the interests and the rights of all. The Emperor Napoleon held his power from the French people. Four times his authority received the popular sanction. In 1814, hereditary right, in the family of the Emperor, was recognized by four millions of votes. Since then the people have not been consulted.

" ' "As the eldest of the nephews of Napoleon, I can then consider myself as the representative of popular election; I will not say of the Empire because in the lapse of twenty years the ideas and wants of France may have changed. But a principle cannot be annulled by facts. It can only be annulled by another principle. Now the principle of popular election in 1804 cannot be annulled by the twelve hundred thousand foreigners who entered France in 1815, nor by the chamber of two hundred and twenty-one deputies in 1830.

" ' "The Napoleon system consists in promoting the march of civilization without disorder and without excess; in giving an impulse to ideas by developing material interests; in strengthening power by rendering it respectable; in disciplining the masses according to their intellectual faculties; in fine, in uniting around the altar of the country the French of all parties by giving them honor and glory as the motives of action."

" ' "No," exclaimed my brave companions in reply, "you shall not die alone. We will die with you, or we will conquer together for the cause of the French people."

" 'You see thus, sir, that it is I who have enticed them, in speaking to them of everything which could move the hearts of Frenchmen. They spoke to me of their oaths. But I reminded them that, in 1815, they had taken the oath to Napoleon II and his dynasty. "Invasion alone," I said to them, "released you from that oath. Well, force can re-establish that which force alone has destroyed." '

"I went even so far as to say to them that the death of the king had been spoken of. I inserted this, my mother, as you will understand, in order to be useful to them. You see how culpable I was in the eyes of the Government. Well, the Government has been generous to me. It has comprehended that my position of exile, that my love for my country, that my relationship to the great man were extenuating causes. Will the jury be less considerate than the Government? Will it not find extenuating causes far stronger in favor of my accomplices, in the souvenirs of the Empire; in the intimate relations of many among them to me; in the enticement of the moment; in the example of Labédoyère; in fine, in that sentiment of generosity which rendered it inevitable that, being soldiers of the Empire, they could not see the eagle without emotion; they preferred to sacrifice their own lives rather than abandon the nephew of the Emperor Napoleon, than to deliver him to his executioners, for we were far from thinking of any mercy in case of failure?"

"In view of Madeira, December 12, 1836.

"I remained ten days at the citadel of Port Louis. Every morning I received a visit from the sub-prefect of Lorient, from the commander of the place, and from the officer of the gendarmerie. They were all very kind to me, and never ceased to speak to me of their attachment to the memory of the Emperor. The commander, Cuynat, and Lieutenant Thiboutot, were unfailing in their attentions to me. I could ever believe myself in the midst of my friends, and the thought that they were in a position hostile to me gave me much pain.

"The winds remained contrary and prevented the frigate from leaving port. At last, on the 21st, a steamer towed out the frigate. The sub-prefect came to tell me that it was time to depart. The drawbridge of the citadel was lowered. I went forth, accompanied by the hospitable officers of the place, in addition to those who brought me to Lorient. I passed between two files of soldiers, who kept off the crowd of the curious, which had gathered to see me.

"We all entered the boats which were to convey us to the frigate, which was waiting for us outside of the harbor. I took leave of these gentlemen with cordiality. I ascended to the deck, and saw with sadness of heart the shores of France disappear behind me.

"I must now give you the details of the frigate. The commander has assigned me a stateroom in the stern of the ship, where I sleep. I dine with him, his son, the second officer, and the aide-de-camp. The commander, captain of the ship, Henry de Villeneuve, is an excellent man, frank and loyal as an old sailor. He pays me every attention. You see that I have much less to complain of than my friends. The other officers of the frigate are also very kind to me.

"There are two other passengers who are two types. The one, an M. D., is a *savant*, twenty-six years of age. He has much intelligence and imagination, mingled with originality, and even with a little eccentricity. For example, he believes in fortune-telling, and undertakes to predict to each one of us his fate. He has also great faith in magnetism, and has told me that a somnambulist had predicted to him, two years ago, that a member of the family of the Emperor would return to France and would dethrone Louis Philippe. He is going to Brazil to make some experiments in electricity. The other passenger is an ancient librarian of Don Pedro, who has preserved all the manners of the ancient court. Maltreated at Brazil, in consequence of his attachment to the Emperor, he returns there to obtain redress.

"The first fifteen days of the voyage were very disagreeable. We were continually tossed about by tempests and by contrary winds, which drove us back almost to the entrance of the Channel. It was impossible during that time to take a single step without clinging to whatever could be seized with one's hand.

"For several days we did not know that our destination was changed. The commander had sealed orders, which he opened and which directed him to go to Rio Janeiro; to remain there as long as should be necessary to re-provision the vessel; to retain me on board during the whole time the frigate remained in the harbor, and then to convey me to New York. Now you know that this frigate was destined to go to the southern seas, where it will remain stationed for two years. It was thus compelled to make an additional voyage of three thousand leagues; for from New York it will be obliged to return to Rio, making a long circuit to the east in order to take advantage of the trade-winds."

"In view of the Canaries, December 14th.

"Every man carries within himself a world, composed of all which he has seen and loved, and to which he returns incessantly, even when he is traversing foreign lands. I do not know, at such times, which is the most painful, the memory of the misfortunes which you have encountered, or of the happy days which are no more. We have passed through the winter and are again in summer. The trade-winds have succeeded the tempests, so that I can spend most of my time on deck. Seated upon the poop, I reflect upon all which has happened to me, and I think of you and of Arenemberg. Situations depend upon the affections which one cherishes. Two months ago I asked only that I might never return to Switzerland. Now, if I should yield to my impressions, I should have no other desire than to find myself again in my little chamber in that beautiful country, where it seems to me that I ought to be so happy. Alas! when one has a soul which feels deeply, one is destined to pass his days in the languor of inaction or in the convulsions of distressing situations.

"When I returned, a few months ago, from conducting Matilde,[1] in entering the park I found a tree broken by the storm, and I said to myself, our marriage will be broken by fate. That which I vaguely imagined has been realized. Have I, then, exhausted in 1836 all the share of happiness which is to be allotted to me?

"Do not accuse me of feebleness if I allow myself to give you an account of all my impressions. One can regret that which he has lost, without repenting of that which he has done. Besides, our sensations are not so independent of interior causes, but that our ideas should be somewhat modified by the objects which surround us. The rays of the sun or the direction of the wind have a great influence over our moral state. When it is beautiful weather, as it is

---

[1] The Princess Matilde, his cousin, daughter of Jerome, with whom it is supposed that he then contemplated marriage.

today, the sea being as calm as the Lake of Constance when we used to walk upon its banks in the evening—when the moon, the same moon, illumines us with the same softened brilliance—when the atmosphere, in fine, is as mild as in the month of August in Europe,—then I am more sad than usual. All memories, pleasant or painful, fall with the same weight upon my heart. Beautiful weather dilates the heart and renders it more impressible, while bad weather contracts it. The passions alone are independent of the changes of the seasons. When we left the barracks of Austerlitz, a flurry of snow fell upon us. Colonel Vaudrey, to whom I made the remark, said to me, 'Notwithstanding this squall, we shall have a fine day.'

"December 29th.

"We passed the line yesterday. The customary ceremony took place. The commander, who is always very polite to me, exempted me from the baptism. It is an ancient usage, but which, nevertheless, is not sensible, to fête the passage of the line by throwing water over one's self and aping a divine office. It was very hot. I have found on board enough books to occupy my time. I have read again the works of M. de Chateaubriand and of J. J. Rousseau. Still, the motion of the ship renders all occupation fatiguing."

"January 1, 1837.

"My dear Mamma, Ma chère Maman,—This is the first day of the year. I am fifteen hundred leagues from you in another hemisphere. Happily, thought traverses that space in less than a second. I am near you. I express to you my profound regret for all the sorrows which I have occasioned you. I renew to you the expression of my tenderness and of my gratitude.

"This morning the officers came in a body to wish me a happy new year. I was much gratified by this attention on their part. At half-past four we were at the table. As we were seventeen degrees of longitude west of Constance, it was at that same time seven o'clock at Arenemberg. You were probably at dinner. I drank, in thought, to your health. You perhaps did the same for me. At least I flattered myself in believing so at that moment. I thought, also, of my companions in misfortune. Alas! I think continually of them. I thought that they were more unhappy than I, and that thought renders me more unhappy than they.

"Present my very tender regards to good Madame Salvage, to the young ladies, to that poor little Clairè, and to M. Cottrau, and to Arsène."

"January 5th.

"We have had a squall, which struck us with extreme violence. If the sails had not been torn to pieces by the wind the frigate would have been in great danger. One of the masts was broken. The rain fell so impetuously that the sea was entirely white. Today the sky is as serene as usual, the damages are repaired, and the tempestuous weather is forgotten. But it is not so with the storms of life. In speaking of the frigate, the commander told me that the frigate which bore your name is now in the South Sea, and is called *La Flora*.

"January 10.

"We have arrived at Rio Janeiro. The *coup d'œil* of the harbor is superb. Tomorrow I shall make a drawing of it. I hope that this letter will soon reach you. Do not think of coming to join me. I do not yet know where I shall settle. Perhaps I may find more inducements to live in South America. The labor to which the uncertainty of my lot will oblige me to devote myself, in order to create for myself a position, will be the only consolation which I can enjoy. Adieu, my mother. Remember me to the old servants, and to our friends of Thurgovia and of Constance. I am very well. Your affectionate and respectful son,

"Louis Napoleon Bonaparte."

Chapter XI
The Death of Hortense, and the Enthronement of her Son

After a short tarry at Rio Janeiro, during which the prince was not permitted to land, the frigate again set sail, and on the 30th of March, 1837, reached Norfolk, Virginia. The prince proceeded immediately to New York. By a cruel error, which has mistaken him for one of his cousins, Pierre Bonaparte, a very wild young man, the reputation of Louis Napoleon has suffered very severely in this country. The evidence is conclusive that there has been a mistake. Louis Napoleon, thoughtful, studious, pensive, has ever been at the farthest possible remove from vulgar dissipation.

A writer in the *Home Journal,* whose reliability is vouched for by the editor, says, in reference to his brief residence in New York: "He is remembered as a quiet, melancholy man, winning esteem rather by the unaffected modesty of his demeanor than by eclât of lineage or the romantic incidents which had befallen him. In the words of a distinguished writer, who well knew him at that day: 'So unostentatious was his deportment, so correct, so pure his life, that even the ripple of scandal cannot appear plausibly upon its surface.' We have inquired of those who entertained him as their guest, of those who tended at his sickbed, of the artist who painted his miniature, of his lady friends (and he was known to some who yet adorn society), of politicians, clergymen, editors, gentlemen of leisure, in fact, of every source whence reliable information could be obtained, and we have gathered but accumulated testimonials to his intrinsic worth and fair fame."

Prince Louis Napoleon remained in this country but seven weeks. The testimony of all who knew him is uncontradicted, that he was peculiarly winning in his attractions as a friend, and irreproachable as a man. Rev. Charles S. Stewart, of the United States Navy, was intimately acquainted with him during the whole period of his residence here. He writes:

"The association was not that of hours only but of days, and on one occasion, at least, of days in succession; and was characterized by a freedom of conversation on a great variety of topics that could scarce fail, under the ingenuousness and frankness of his manner, to put me in possession of his views, principles, and feelings upon most points that give insight to character.

"I never heard a sentiment from him and never witnessed a feeling that could detract from his honor and purity as a man, or his dignity as a prince. On the contrary, I often had occasion to admire the lofty thought and exalted conceptions which seemed most to occupy his mind. He was winning in the invariableness of his amiability, often playful in spirits and manner, and warm in his affections. He was a most fondly attached son and seemed to idolize his mother. When speaking of her, the intonations of his voice and his whole manner were often as gentle and feminine as those of a woman.

"In both eating and drinking he was, as far as I observed, abstemious rather than self-indulgent. I repeatedly breakfasted, dined, and supped in his company; and never knew him to partake of anything stronger in drink than the light wines of France and Germany, and of these in great moderation. I have been with him early and late, unexpectedly as well as by appointment, and never saw reason for the slightest suspicion of any irregularity in his habits."

Such is the testimony, so far as can be ascertained, of everyone who enjoyed any personal acquaintance with Louis Napoleon while in this country. He was the guest of Washington Irving, Chancellor Kent, and of the Hamiltons, Clintons, Livingstons, and other such distinguished families in New York.

While busily engaged in studying the institutions of our country and making arrangements for quite an extensive tour through the States, he received a letter from his mother which immediately changed all his plans. The event is thus described by Mr. Stewart:

"With this expectation he consulted me and others as to the arrangement of the route of travel, so as to visit the different sections of the Union at the most desirable seasons. But his plans were suddenly changed by intelligence of the serious illness of Queen Hortense, or, as then styled, the Duchess of St. Leu. I was dining with him the day the letter conveying this information was received. Recognizing the writing on the envelope, as it was handed to him at

Hortense

the table, he hastily broke the seal and had scarce glanced over half a page before he exclaimed:

" 'My mother is ill, I must see her. Instead of a tour of the States, I shall take the next packet for England. I will apply for passports for the Continent at every embassy in London, and if unsuccessful, will make my way to her without them.' "

The following was the letter which he received from his mother:

"My dear Son,—I am about to submit to an operation which has become absolutely necessary. If it is not successful I send you, by this letter, my benediction. We shall meet again, shall we not? in a better world, where may you come to join me as late as possible. In leaving this world I have but one regret; it is to leave you and your affectionate tenderness—the greatest charm of my existence here. It will be a consolation to you, my dear child, to reflect that by your attentions you have rendered your mother as happy as it was possible for her, in her circumstances, to be. Think that a loving and a watchful eye still rests on the dear ones we leave behind, and that we shall surely meet again. Cling to this sweet idea. It is too necessary not to be true. I press you to my heart, my dear son. I am very calm and resigned, and hope that we shall again meet in this world. Your affectionate mother,

"Hortense.

"Arenemberg, April 3, 1837."

As we have mentioned, Queen Hortense, upon receiving news of the arrest of her son, hastened to France to do what she could to save him. Madame Récamier found her at Viry, in great anguish of spirit. When she received tidings of his banishment she returned, overwhelmed with the deepest grief, to her desolated home. It seems that even then an internal disease, which, with a mother's love, she had not revealed to her son, was threatening her life. Madame Récamier, as she bade her adieu, was much moved by the great change in her appearance. The two friends never met again.

Madame Salvage, a distinguished lady, who had devoted herself with lifelong enthusiasm to the Queen of Holland, accompanied her to France and returned with her to Arenemberg. On the 13th of April, Madame Salvage wrote the following letter from Arenemberg to Madame Récamier.

"I wrote you a long letter four days ago, dear friend, telling you of my unhappiness. I received yesterday your letter of the 7th, for which I thank you. I needed it much, and it is a consolation to me.

"I have informed Madame, the Duchess of St. Leu, of the lively interest you take in her troubles, and have given her your message. She was much touched by it, even to tears; and has begged me several times to tell you how much she appreciated it.

"I have not replied to you sooner, because I hoped to give you better tidings. Alas! it is quite the contrary. After a consultation of the physicians of Constance and Zurich with Dr. Conneau, her own physician, Professor Lisfranc, from Paris, was called in, on account of his skill, and also because he is the recognized authority with regard to the operation two of these gentlemen thought necessary.

"After a careful examination, the opinion of M. Lisfranc and that of the three other consulting physicians was, that the operation was impossible. They were unanimous in pronouncing an irrevocable sentence, and they have left us no hope in human resources. I still like to trust in the infinite goodness of God, whom I implore with earnest prayers.

"The mind of madame the duchess is as calm as one could expect in a position like hers. They told her that they would not perform the operation because it was not necessary, and because a mere treatment would suffice, with time and patience, to produce a perfect cure. She had been quite resigned to submit to the operation, showing a noble courage. Now she is happy in not being obliged to undergo it, and is filled with hope.

"In anticipation of the operation, of which, against my advice, she had been told a fortnight before M. Lisfranc came, she made her will and attended to the last duties of religion.

"On the 30th of March, an hour after she had partaken of the communion, she had the joy, which she looked upon as a divine favor, of receiving a large package from her son, the first since the departure from Lorient. His letter, which is very long, contains a relation of all he has done, all that has happened to him, and much that he has felt since he left Arenemberg, until he wrote, the 10th of January, on board the frigate *Andromeda* lying in the harbor of Rio Janeiro, where he was not permitted to go on shore. He had on board M. de Chateaubriand's works, and reread them during a frightful storm that lasted a fortnight, and allowed of no other occupation, and scarcely that. Pray tell this to M. de Chateaubriand, in recalling me personally to his kind remembrance.

"Think of me sometimes. Think of my painful position. To give to a person whom we love, and whom we are soon to lose, a care that is perfectly ineffectual; to seek to alleviate sharp and almost continual suffering, and only succeed very imperfectly; to wear a calm countenance when the heart is torn; to deceive, to try unceasingly to inspire hopes that we no longer cherish,—ah, believe me, this is frightful, and one would cheerfully give up life itself. Adieu, dear friend, you know how I love you."

Louis Napoleon, hastening to the bedside of his dying mother, took ship from New York for London. The hostility of the allied powers to him was such that it was with great difficulty he could reach Arenemberg. He arrived there just in time to receive the dying blessing of his mother and to close her eyes in death. Just before she died, Hortense assembled all her household in the dying chamber. She took each one affectionately by the hand and addressed to each one a few words of adieu. Her son, her devoted physician Dr. Conneau, and the ladies of her household, bathed in tears, were kneeling by her bedside. Her mind, in delirious dreams, had again been with the Emperor, sympathizing with him in the terrible tragedy of his fall. But now, as death drew near, reason was fully restored. "I have never," said she, "done wrong to anyone. God will have mercy upon me." Conscious that the final moment had arrived, she made an effort to throw her arms around the neck of her son in a mother's last embrace, when she fell, back upon her pillow dead. It was October 5, 1837.

The prince, with his own hands, closed his mother's eyes in that sleep which knows no earthly waking. He remained for some time upon his knees at her bedside, with his weeping eyes buried in his hands. At last he was led away from the precious remains from which it seemed impossible for him to separate himself. His home and his heart were indeed desolate. Motherless, with neither brother nor sister, his aged and infirm father dying in Italy, where he could not be permitted to visit him, banished from his native land, jealously watched and menaced by all the allied powers, his fair name maligned, all these considerations seemed to fill his cup of sorrow to the brim.

It was the dying wish of Hortense that she might be buried by the side of Josephine, her mother, in the village church of Ruel, near Malmaison. The Government of Louis Philippe, which had closed the gates of France against Hortense while living, allowed her lifeless remains to sleep beneath her native soil. But the son was not permitted to follow his mother to her grave. It was feared that his appearance in France would rouse the enthusiasm of the masses; that they would rally around him, and, sweeping away the throne of Louis Philippe in a whirlwind of indignation, would re-establish the Empire. Madame Récamier, speaking of the death of Hortense, says:

"After the unfortunate attempt of Prince Louis, grief, anxiety and perhaps the loss of a last and secret hope, put an end to the turbulent existence of one who was little calculated to lead such a life of turmoil. France, closed to her living, was open to her dead, and she was carried to Ruel and laid beside her mother. A funeral service was celebrated in her honor at the village church. All the relics of the Empire were there; among them the widow of Murat,[1] who there witnessed the ceremony that shortly afterwards was to be performed over herself.

"It was winter. A thick snow covered the ground. The landscape was as silent and cold as the dead herself. I gave sincere tears to this woman so gracious and so kind; and I learned shortly afterwards that she had remembered me in her will. It is not without a profound and a religious emotion that we receive these remembrances from friends who are no more; these pledges of affection which come to you, so to say, from across the tomb, as if to assure you that thoughts of you had followed them as far as there. Judge, then, how touched I was in receiving the legacy destined for me—that light, elegant, and mysterious gift, chosen to recall to me unceasingly the tie that had existed between us. It was a lace veil, the one she wore the day of our meeting in St. Peter's."

---

[1] Caroline Bonaparte.

In reference to the mother and the son, Julie de Marguerittes writes: "Louis Napoleon's love for his mother had in it a tenderness and devotion even beyond that of a son. She had been his instructor and companion; and from the hour of her change of position she had manifested great and noble qualities, which the frivolity and prosperity of a court might forever have left unrevealed. Hortense was a woman to be loved and revered. And even at this distance of years, Napoleon's love for his mother has suffered no change. He has striven, in all ways, to associate her with his present high fortune. He has made an air of her composition, *Partant pour la Syrie,* the national air of France. The ship which bore him from Marseilles to Genoa, on his Italian expedition, is called *La Reine Hortense,* after his mother."

Scarcely were the remains of Hortense committed to the tomb, ere the Swiss Government received an imperative command from the Government of Louis Philippe to banish Louis Napoleon from the soil of Switzerland. To save the country which had so kindly adopted him from war, the prince retired to London. He could have no hopes of regaining his rights as a French citizen until the Government of Louis Philippe should be overthrown. Another attempt was made at Boulogne in August, 1840. It proved a failure. Louis Napoleon was again arrested, tried, and condemned to imprisonment for life. Six years he passed in dreary captivity in the Castle of Ham. The following brief account of the wonderful escape of the prince is given in his own words, contained in a letter to the editor of the *Journal de la Somme.*

"My dear M. de George,—My desire to see my father once more in this world made me attempt the boldest enterprise I ever engaged in. It required more resolution and courage on my part than at Strasburg or Boulogne; for I was determined not to bear the ridicule that attaches to those who are arrested escaping under a disguise, and a failure I could not have endured. The following are the particulars of my escape:

"You know that the fort was guarded by four hundred men, who furnished daily sixty soldiers, placed as sentries outside the walls. Moreover, the principal gate of the prison was guarded by three jailers, two of whom were constantly on duty. It was necessary that I should first elude their vigilance, afterwards traverse the inside court before the windows of the commandant's residence, and arriving there, I should be obliged to pass by a gate which was guarded by soldiers.

"Not wishing to communicate my design to anyone, it was necessary to disguise myself. As several of the rooms in the building I occupied were undergoing repairs, it was not difficult to assume the dress of a workman. My good and faithful valet, Charles Thelin, procured a smock-frock and a pair of wooden shoes, and after shaving off my mustaches I took a plank upon my shoulders.

"On Monday morning I saw the workmen enter at half-past eight o'clock. Charles took them some drink, in order that I should not meet any of them on my passage. He was also to call one of the turnkeys while Dr. Conneau conversed with the others. Nevertheless I had scarcely got out of my room before I was accosted by a workman who took me for one of his comrades; and at the bottom of the stairs I found myself in front of the keeper. Fortunately, I placed the plank I was carrying before my face, and succeeded in reaching the yard. Whenever I passed a sentinel or any other person I always kept the plank before my face.

"Passing before the first sentinel, I let my pipe fall and stopped to pick up the bits. There I met the officer on duty; but as he was reading a letter he did not pay attention to me. The soldiers at the guard-house appeared surprised at my dress, and a drummer turned around several times to look at me. I placed the plank before my face, but they appeared to be so curious that I thought I should never escape them until I heard them cry, 'Oh, it is Bernard!'

"Once outside, I walked quickly towards the road of St. Quentin. Charles, who the day before had engaged a carriage, shortly overtook me, and we arrived at St. Quentin. I passed through the town on foot, after having thrown off my smock-frock. Charles procured a post-chaise, under pretext of going to Cambrai. We arrived without meeting with any hindrance at Valenciennes, where I took the railway. I had procured a Belgian passport, but nowhere was I asked to show it.

"During my escape, Dr. Conneau, always so devoted to me, remained in prison, and caused them to believe that I was ill, in order to give me time to reach the frontier. It was necessary to be convinced that the Government would never set me at liberty if I would not consent to dishonor myself, before I could be persuaded to quit France. It was also a matter of duty that I should exert all my powers to be able to console my father in his old age.

"Adieu, my dear M. de George. Although free, I feel myself to be most unhappy. Receive the assurance of my sincere friendship; and if you are able, endeavor to be useful to my kind Conneau."

It was the latter part of May, 1846, that Louis Napoleon escaped from Ham. He repaired immediately to London. In accordance with his habits and his tastes, he continued to devote himself earnestly to his studies, still cherishing the unfaltering opinion that he was yet to be the Emperor of France. In London he was cordially welcomed by his old friends, Count d'Orsay and Lady Blessington. His cousin Maria of Baden, then Lady Douglass, subsequently the Duchess of Hamilton, was proud to receive him in her sumptuous abode, and to present him to her aristocratic friends. To her, it is said that he confided his projects and hopes more frankly than to anyone else. In one of his notes he wrote,

"MY DEAR COUSIN,—I do not belong to myself, I belong to my name and my country. It is because my fortune has twice betrayed me, that my destiny is nearer its accomplishment. I bide my time."

In the latter part of February, 1848, the throne of Philippe was overturned, and he fled from France. Louis Napoleon immediately returned to Paris after so many weary years of exile. This is not the place to describe the scenes which ensued. It is sufficient simply to state that, almost by acclamation, he was sent by the people of Paris to the Assembly, was there elected president of the Republic, and then, by nearly eight million of votes, the Empire was re-established and Louis Napoleon was placed upon the imperial throne.

As soon as Louis Napoleon was chosen president of the French Republic, Walter Savage Landor, a brilliant scholar, a profound, original thinker, and a highly independent and honorable man, wrote as follows to Lady Blessington, under date of January 9th, 1849:

"Possibly you may have never seen the two articles which I enclose. I inserted another in the *Examiner,* deprecating the anxieties which a truly patriotic and, in my opinion, a singularly wise man, was about to encounter, in accepting the presidency of France. Necessity will compel him to assume the imperial power, to which the voice of the army and of the people will call him. You know, who know not merely my writings but my heart, how little I care for station. I may therefore tell you safely, that I feel a great interest, a great anxiety for the welfare of Louis Napoleon. I told him that if he were ever again in prison, I would visit him there, but never if he were upon a throne would I come near him. He is the only man living who would adorn one. But thrones are my aversion and abhorrence. France, I fear, can exist in no other condition. May God protect the virtuous Louis Napoleon, and prolong in happiness the days of my dear kind friend Lady Blessington.

"WALTER SAVAGE LANDOR.

"P.S.—I wrote a short letter to the President, and not of congratulation. May he find many friends as disinterested and sincere."

Even the blunt Duke of Wellington wrote as follows to the Count d'Orsay under date of April 9, 1849: "I rejoice at the prosperity of France and of the success of the president of the Republic. Everything tends towards the permanent tranquility of Europe," which is necessary for the happiness of all.

If Hortense from the spirit-land can look down upon her son, her heart must be cheered in view of the honors which his native land, with such unprecedented unanimity, has conferred upon him. And still more must her heart be cheered in view of the many, many years of peace, prosperity, and happiness which France has enjoyed under his reign. Every well-informed man will admit that the kingdom of France has never, since its foundations were laid, enjoyed so many years of tranquility, and of mental and material advancement at home, and also of respect and influence abroad, as during the reign of the son of Hortense.

The Emperor is eminently happy in his domestic relations. There are none who know the Empress Eugénie who do not revere and love her. She is the worthy successor of Josephine, upon the throne of the reinstated empire. The following beautiful tribute to her virtues comes from the lips of our former distinguished ambassador at the court of France, Hon. John A. Dix. They were uttered in a speech which he addressed to the American residents in Paris, upon the occasion of his surrendering the ambassadorial chair to his successor, Hon. Mr. Washburne. It was in June, 1869.

"Of her who is the sharer of the Emperor's honors and the companion of his toils—who in the hospital, at the altar, or on the throne is alike exemplary in the discharge of her varied duties, whether incident to her position, or voluntarily taken upon herself, it is difficult for me to speak without rising above the level of the common language of eulogism.

"But I am standing here today, as a citizen of the United States, without official relations to my own Government, or any other. I have taken my leave of the imperial family, and I know no reason why I may not freely speak what I honestly think; especially as I know I can say nothing which will not find a cordial response in your own breasts.

"As in the history of the ruder sex, great luminaries have from time to time risen high above the horizon, to break and at the same time to illustrate, the monotony of the general movement,—so in the annals of hers, brilliant lights have at intervals shone forth, and shed their luster upon the stately march of regal pomp and power.

"When I have seen her taking part in the most imposing of all imperial pageants—the opening of the Legislative Chambers—standing amid the assembled magistracy of Paris, surrounded by the representatives of the talent, the genius, and the piety of this great empire; or amidst the resplendent scenes of the palace, moving about with a gracefulness all her own, and with a simplicity of manner which has a double charm when allied to exalted rank and station, I confess that I have more than once whispered to myself, and I believe not always inaudibly, the beautiful verse of the graceful and courtly Claudian, the last of the Roman poets,

" '*Divino semitu, gressu claruit;*'

"or, rendered in our own plain English, and stripped of its poetic hyperbole, '*The very path she treads is radiant with her unrivaled step.*'"

THE END.

CPSIA information can be obtained
at www.ICGtesting.com
Printed in the USA
LVHW022333010920
664770LV00013B/1682